AF594725

The OSTERIA PAPAVERO COOKBOOK

RECIPES FROM THE ITALIAN SHACK AND BEYOND

FRANCESCO MANGANO
and LINDSAY CHRISTIANS

PHOTOGRAPHY BY SUNNY FRANTZ

LITTLE CREEK PRESS
AND BOOK DESIGN
MINERAL POINT, WISCONSIN

Copyright © 2023 by Francesco Mangano and Lindsay Christians
Photo copyright © 2023 Sunny Frantz

All rights reserved. No part of this publication may be reproduced, distributed, or transmitted in any form or by any means, including photocopying, recording, digital scanning, or other electronic or mechanical methods, without the prior written permission of the publisher, except in the case of brief quotations embodied in critical reviews and certain other noncommercial uses permitted by copyright law. For permission requests or other information, please send correspondence to the following address:

Little Creek Press
5341 Sunny Ridge Road
Mineral Point, WI 53565

ORDERING INFORMATION
Quantity sales. Special discounts are available on quantity purchases by corporations, associations, and others. For details, contact info@littlecreekpress.com

Orders by US trade bookstores and wholesalers.
Please contact Little Creek Press or Ingram for details.

Printed in the United States of America

Cataloging-in-Publication Data
Names: Mangano, Francesco, and Christians, Lindsay, authors
Title: The Osteria Papavero Cookbook. Recipes from the Italian Shack and Beyond
Description: Mineral Point, WI: Little Creek Press, 2023
Identifiers: LCCN: 2023903999 | ISBN: 978-1-955656-46-7
Subjects: COOKING / Regional & Ethnic / Italian

Book design by Little Creek Press

Cover photo: Sunny Frantz

"Life is a combination of pasta and magic"

—Federico Fellini

"Listen to the beauty of repose, of reawakening, and of your appetite. Look for the time of the sun and the light of the moon. Build tables and chairs so you will never be alone, aware that the art of nourishing others with your own solitude teaches friendship."

—"Papale Papale: Thoughts and Recipes to Nourish your Soul" by Fabio Picchi

TABLE OF CONTENTS

About this Book. 7

About these Recipes 9

Introduction 10

An Ingredient Primer 14

La Pianura: The Plains (Bologna) 17

La Montagna: The Mountains (The Dolomites) 47

Il Mare: The Sea (Castiglioncello) 59

The Farmers' Market: Madison, Wisconsin 77

La Dispensa: The Pantry 94

Acknowledgments 98

About the Authors 99

Index 100

Osteria
Papavero

ABOUT THIS BOOK

Osteria Papavero has been around for 17 years at 128 E. Wilson St. in downtown Madison, during which we've had fun with so many different kinds of foods and preparations.

But overall, at Papavero, I don't stray too much from what Italian food is, and what Italian recipes and techniques are. I don't believe in inventing—I believe in crafting, not creating new things. And not everything is made from scratch. Some things we make, like stuffed pasta, and some things we buy from Italy, like dried pasta and certain cured meats.

One common trait remains: the commitment never to waste. It has become almost a fad to talk about "sustainability." At Papavero, we applied this "no waste" concept from the very start of operations. A fennel frond or a cauliflower stem might become—after cooking, blending and straining overnight—a beautiful base for a pasta filling. Meat poached in stock to make a broth becomes the base for a tortellini filling the following day. And hazelnut paste leftover from ice cream making becomes a quick pesto, with basil, garlic and good Parmigiano.

In kitchens across the country, the chef's ego and desire to surprise the customer comes before respect for the product. I hope that from these years spent in Madison that my cooks will take away these things from my kitchen: Be humble. Don't waste. And respect the product.

Narrowing down these recipes was tough. Beyond the three or four dozen recipes that customers see on the menu each week, there are recipes we make regularly and specials that we create by matching farmers' market produce to Italian recipes. That changes every weekday. If I had to do a computation of all the recipes we've done in 16 years, it would probably be in the thousands. And some omissions were obvious—our charcuterie would require another book. (Cured meats can take years to finish curing.)

So yes, there are recipes you may want in a Papavero cookbook that we have not been able to include here. We have shared as many as we can, and we hope you enjoy them.

ABOUT THESE RECIPES

We have aimed to make this book easy to use for home cooks. That means you will see volume and weight measures in some recipes, particularly in the baking recipes where using a scale will be helpful. You'll also see a mix of grams and ounces, based on how home cooks purchase things in the United States.

Most of these are weeknight recipes. When there are more esoteric ingredients, such as octopus, wild boar, spinach pasta or barley malt, we've given tips on where to find them, with a focus on Midwestern resources.

Italian recipes are forgiving! If you have a few extra ounces in the pan, it usually won't make a difference. They are rustic for a reason.

Most of these recipes don't require specialized tools, but a few will help. Among them are a food processor, a blender, a stand mixer, a tomato/potato ricer (preferably stainless steel), a zester and a fine-mesh sieve or chinois. If you want to try the pasta recipes, you will need a pasta roller, a pasta cutter and a rolling pin.

These recipes were adapted from a restaurant kitchen and tested in home kitchens. We have done our best to translate them, culturally and practically. As cooks at Papavero know, the best indicators are your own senses. Listen, smell, look at and taste your food as it cooks, and trust yourself.

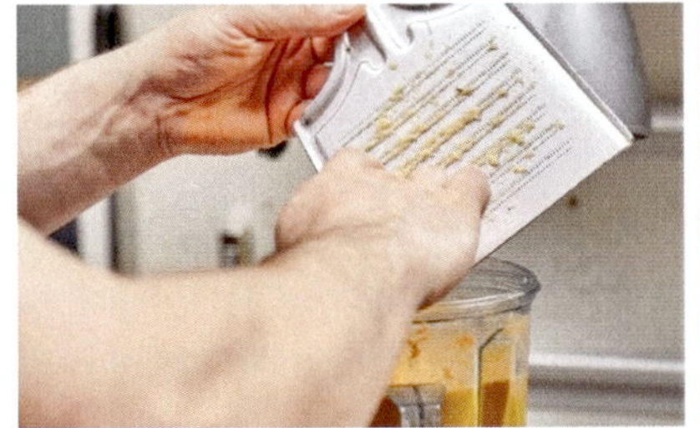

INTRODUCTION

I grew up in Bologna, which some call the capital of food in Italy. Bologna is home to salumi, mortadella, Parmigiano and tortellini in brodo. It produces some of the finest meats and cheeses in the world.

Yet my world, growing up in Bologna, was shaped by more than the food of the Italian plains. As a child, I spent summers by the sea in a little town called Castiglioncello on the Tuscan coast, with my grandfather Vincenzo Buffa and my grandmother Celide (or Iris, as her sisters called her). This is where I have my earliest food memories.

Castiglioncello, a little touristy town of fewer than four thousand people, is where my mom's side of the family would gather during the traditional Catholic holidays of Christmas and Easter. As they prepared for the feast, my aunts would make the pasta dough, rolling it thin enough to be stuffed and shaped into tortellini. I have memories of being 7 or 8 years old and using the pasta machine, because they trusted me with a hand crank. I couldn't fold or shape the pasta, but cranking, I could do.

While my aunts stretched and filled, my Uncle Enzo would be cleaning and slow-braising wild game he'd caught during the week in the Tuscan countryside—wild boar, pheasants, grouse, wild hare. My other Uncle Renzo (yes, Enzo and Renzo!) would bring over chicken liver crostini, the same kind his own mother had been making for years.

This work was all preparation for the family to put "feet under the table" for many hours. (That expression came in handy years later, during my teenage nocturnal escapades with friends in the trattorie and osterie of Bologna.)

Imagine starting a meal with a plate of crostini with different toppings, plus sliced cold meats and fresh bread from the local bakery. Then move on, leisurely, to different pastas, always at least one stuffed, as well as a game ragout or meaty Bolognese.

Is that it? No! Roasted meats and bollito misto (boiled meats) would come next, with different sauces to accompany them—salsa verde, salsa rosa, salsa agrodolce. Then there would be a salad, or some cooked bitter greens at Easter. My cousin Luca, my Aunt Carla's son, is a great baker (Nigella Lawson is his inspirational baking goddess). He would bring usually two or three desserts, the more the better.

Beyond Luca's sweets, at Christmas there would be panettone (fruit cake) and pandoro (sweet bread). At Easter, we'd have the classic colomba, a leavened, sugar-coated, almond-topped sweet bread. Then ice cream and fresh fruit.

We were not finished. Coffee and amaro (Italian bitters) would be served around the table, but only after my Uncle Enzo passed around the artisanal cheeses he had purchased from the local farmers or formaggiai (cheesemongers). Various types of pecorino would often be center stage in this selection.

Several recipes in this book have roots in those family feasts. Here, you'll find inspiration for crostini toppings, like eggplant caponata **(page 79)**, and pastas, like my Aunt Carla's zucchini pasta with ricotta and basil **(page 67)**.

I have recreated my Uncle Enzo's wild boar ragout **(page 74)** and provided instructions for meat tortelli **(page 28)**, a filled pasta that's a holiday staple. Insalata rifatta, or a cold beef salad **(page 63)**, could be made with the leftover roast from a big family dinner, one served, of course, with salsa verde **(page 96)**.

Beyond the feasts, many recipes are tied to my childhood. I remember going to the bakery with my mom in the morning for fresh-baked products and fried flatbread, gnocco fritto, which we serve at the restaurant now. They'd have crescente (Bologna's own type of focaccia) with salumi scraps, like prosciutto (a Barese-style focaccia with tomatoes is on **page 18**).

I grew up in a town called San Pietro that was close to the big city, but still 20 miles away. Back then it was probably ten thousand people, but there were some 20 restaurants, three bakeries and one pastry shop, and at least four or five gelateria. (It was a lot for ten thousand!) Gelato is a memory-lane kind of thing for me. (The sour cream ice cream **(page 92)** from our pastry chef Susan Cesnik is a very easy way to start making your own desserts, before moving onto the iconic Papavero budino **(page 86)**.

We didn't only vacation on the coast. From an early age, my Uncle Renzo and Aunt Laura brought me along on camping trips to locations in the Italian alps that would change from year to year. The Dolomites earned a special place in my heart. My recipes from that region, like wild mushroom stew **(page 48)** and goulasch **(page 52)**, share similar qualities with dishes in nearby Germany.

I learned to cook some things early—I remember making vegetable gratins when I was 11 or 12, blanching the vegetables, making a béchamel, putting Parmigiana on top and baking it. Our recipe for fennel gratin **(page 30)** will prove how simple this is.

My culinary and professional training informed these recipes as well. After graduating from the University of Bologna in 1998, earning a culinary degree at Madison College and spending three years in Wisconsin,

I returned to Italy with my then-wife in 2002. The intention was to seek a position at a good restaurant in Bologna while my wife translated her pharmacy degree to work in Italy.

In addition to restaurant work, I decided to pursue more education, this time a master's degree in Food and Wine Tourism and Promotion of Local Products from the University of Siena and Arezzo in Tuscany. It was a yearlong intensive, launched by the same people who created Slow Food's University of Gastronomic Sciences only a few years later.

This degree was a game changer. I have always been a curious person, but the opportunity to meet every week with butchers, chefs, agronomists and farmers, all there to give lectures, was very exciting. I would study all weekend, learning from experts about honey, olive oil, chocolate and more, then hop a three-hour train ride home to work all week in a restaurant.

In 2004, we returned to Madison, and I continued to learn as we made plans for Papavero. The carrot ginger soup (page 85) was passed on by one of my mentors. I began to adapt Italian recipes for local tastes, like cured swordfish (page 60) and our local version of a panino pazzo, or a "crazy sandwich" (page 82). The mushrooms I foraged in Wisconsin and the vegetables grown here became essential to translating Italian dishes for Wisconsin diners.

This book is for my restaurant. From day one, we've had people asking for different recipes—the boar, the budino, the lasagna. Even the simplest things people will ask, like how do we make the tomato butter sauce? (Good quality tomatoes and butter. That's it!) One or two months will go by without a question, and then someone will come in and say, "How do you do the crespelle? I have never made that before."

I wanted to put together recipes that are staples for us, the dishes people come for every year, that don't come off the menu. This is your opportunity to use our recipes and to try them at home.

And there was another, more personal reason I wanted to write this book. I took a lot of time away from my kids over the past 16 years. They went through a divorce, and I think they have been suffering unwillingly because I spent so much time in the kitchen. Sometimes I'd realize a week had gone by and I'd only seen them a couple of nights or afternoons.

I wrote this book because I want to give my kids something they can use in their own homes in the future, maybe 30 years from now, when I'm not around anymore. So they can remember: These are the flavors my dad was cooking in the restaurant. I want to leave them something written—something that my uncle and my mom never left me.

This book is for my family. The life of a chef is not an easy one.

AN INGREDIENT PRIMER

Balsamic Vinegar

"Aceto balsamico tradizionale" is traditional balsamic vinegar from the cities of Modena and Reggio Emilia in Italy. This is, quite frankly, the only type of balsamic vinegar to buy. Other balsamic vinegars are often darkened not by natural aging in wood barrels, but with caramel solutions.

Chocolate

Look for French or Italian chocolate with at least 70% cocoa content. Our cocoa powder of choice is Valrhona.

Cured Meats

We have made our own salumi at Papavero since 2006. Purchase cured meats that are Italian-made, especially in the case of speck and mortadella, which are very difficult to perfect due to the many laborious steps in the production and the variety of details in order to achieve a good product.

Eggs

Papavero uses large eggs.

Milk and Cream

When a recipe calls for milk, please use only whole (full-fat) milk.

Olive Oil

Use extra-virgin olive oil in these recipes. Italian brands are available at specialty shops like Fraboni's in Monona or Glorioso's in Milwaukee.

Pasta/Gnocchi

All of our stuffed pastas are made in house, and are typically just a combination of eggs and all-purpose flour. With the exception of egg pappardelle, we purchase most pasta from Italy. Given the high volume of sales of gnocchi at Papavero, we don't always make fresh gnocchi from scratch, choosing instead to order good-quality imported gnocchi from Italy.

I do not believe in pasta extruders sold at cheap prices, even when we're talking about a couple of thousand dollars. Pasta making is an art, and a very old one. It combines human knowledge and good products from nature, like wheat flour, with machinery that is appropriate for the task. Then add natural phenomena such as wind (for drying the pasta slowly, though nowadays that process is sped up) and time.

It's foolish to think that you can replicate all of these elements to perfection, even in a modern kitchen full of gadgets. We can all find excellent pasta, dried and fresh, at local specialty shops and online.

If you don't want to make your own lasagna sheets, look for them (preferably green, which means they are made with spinach) in local shops that carry Italian products, such as Fraboni's.

Salt

At Papavero, we use both kosher (coarse) salt and fine sea salt. Any brand of kosher salt will do; we use it only to salt cooking water for pasta or vegetables. For fine sea salt, a variety of good brands can be found at shops like Orange Tree Imports in Madison.

Sugar

We use fine granulated white sugar in our kitchen. Certain recipes, like the one for butterscotch pudding, or when we're preparing a brine for fish or meat, might call for dark brown sugar. We don't use powdered sugar very often, typically only to sweeten whipping cream or to dust some on cakes before plating.

Tomatoes

Our canned tomatoes of choice are San Marzano, preferably from Italy. San Marzano tomatoes tend to have fewer seeds and a thinner skin, which makes them ideal for sauce making.

Vanilla Beans

Make sure when buying fresh vanilla beans that they are still pliable and not dried out. Store in a double Ziploc® bag to prevent drying. Find them at most grocery stores and baking shops.

LA PIANURA

THE PLAINS (BOLOGNA)

I love Sundays. I always have. In my family, Sunday was, of course, for church, but it was also for many other things. Sunday was one of only two days when I could have lunch with both my mom and dad, who worked in downtown Bologna Monday through Friday. (He eventually retired after 35 years of working for the same phone company as an accountant.)

During the 10-minute walk from my house to the church at the center of town, I could "reroute" and get a chance to peek in the window of the most renowned pastry shop in San Pietro, Pasticceria Chiari.

My parents, being careful with spending, wouldn't take me there unless it was a special occasion, but that glass display of pastries would make anyone salivate. It was full of eclairs ("bigne") filled with hazelnut and chocolate, truffle-style chocolate "bombes" with crisp outsides and rum inside, and zabaglione "millefeuille," probably my favorite puff pastry confection and the subject of many of my dreams.

"Pianura" simply means flatland, or valley. The cuisine of this place includes the Barese-style focaccia that my dad would eat as a child, as well as the biove bread and gnocco fritto I would see every morning at the bakery.

I've passed on a love for lasagna to my kids, made with bechamel and Bolognese ragout. I have recipes for them all here. Tortellini, or tortelli, you'd find at festivals but also at 99% of restaurants around Bologna. Fennel or cauliflower in bechamel is something you'd find every fall at trattoria, those less expensive, more rustic places to eat. Gnocchi with radicchio and smoked prosciutto, or speck, is also a fall dish.

This collection of recipes is pretty representative of what food is like in Bologna. This food is flavorful but also pretty heavy if you eat it all year long. If you travel to Italy and you spend a few days in Bologna, you may want to go somewhere else like Tuscany, with lighter food options such as Tuscan kale, beans and seafood. At Papavero, when people order crespelle in August, I laugh because it's such a heavy dish! When it's hot outside, that dish is a killer.

BARESE-STYLE FOCACCIA

(SAVORY ITALIAN BREAD)

YIELDS 1 round, medium-sized loaf

When I was about 7 years old, my dad started taking me along on his yearly trips to the region of Puglia, where his parents raised him until he was 18. My first memories of focaccia are linked to these trips, and to my paternal grandfather's tiny piece of land where he grew his own olive, fig and almond trees. I will always associate this bread with lunches spent sitting on the ground in the shade of those ancient olive trees, drenched by the Apulian sun.

If you know and love focaccia, this recipe may be different than what you expect. There are dozens of focaccia styles across Italy, and the Barese style is a little denser because of the potato. Don't stress too much about the starter, which can be tricky to measure. You're adding it to give the yeast a little boost, but it's not necessary.

1 cup (150 grams) cherry tomatoes

Dried oregano

1 cup (167 grams) semolina flour

1 cup (125 grams) all-purpose flour

1 cup (126 grams) riced or grated cooked potatoes (see note)

1/4 cup (57 grams) homemade bread starter (50/50 mix of flour and water, optional; see headnote)

2 teaspoons barley malt syrup

2 teaspoons fine sea salt

2 tablespoons (24 grams) instant yeast

2 tablespoons olive oil, plus more for the top

1 cup lukewarm water

Grease the bottom and sides of a 10-inch round baking pan with high sides, at least 3 inches. Halve the cherry tomatoes, sprinkle them with salt, and let them sit for about 15 to 20 minutes. Before you use them, drain the tomatoes and season with dried oregano.

Place the flours, riced potatoes, starter (if using), barley malt, sea salt, instant yeast, olive oil and lukewarm water into the bowl of a stand mixer with a dough hook attachment. Mix these together for about 12 minutes, or until the dough looks supple but not too sticky.

Transfer the dough to a counter and gently shape into a ball. Transfer to the greased pan. Cover the dough with greased plastic wrap or parchment paper and let rise for about 20 minutes.

With lightly oiled hands, smoosh the dough down and spread it into the edges of the pan. Top the dough with drained cherry tomatoes. Sprinkle the dough with a pinch of dried oregano and more extra-virgin olive oil. Leave the dough uncovered and let it double in size. This usually takes about an hour, but may be less depending on the temperature of your kitchen and the freshness of your starter. When it doubles, it's ready.

Heat your oven to 450°F. Bake until the tops of the focaccia look light brown and the bread pulls away from the edges of the baking pan, about 20 minutes. Serve warm.

CHEF'S NOTE: Boil or microwave about 1 pound of potatoes, then use a box grater or ricer to break them down.

CHEF'S NOTE: If your dough seems dry, add a little bit of tomato sauce to the tomatoes and oregano.

BIOVE BREAD

(SOFT ITALIAN BREAD)

YIELDS about 1 1/2 pounds of bread, or 2 large rolls

If you were a little kid in Italy in the 1980s—let's say elementary school age—and you lived in a small town with the luxury of three outstanding bakeries, chances were good that you'd be sent to school in the morning with a packed lunch of biove bread and Nutella or mortadella. For me, it was usually the latter.

Biove is a quick, soft bread made with simple pantry ingredients. Americans may get squeamish about lard, but it's an important ingredient in Bologna because of the long tradition of pig farming in central Italy. It's used more often in bread than olive oil. This bread has three times the amount of lard than you'll find in typical breads, which keeps it moist.

Look for lard from a local farmer, or Epic Provisions also makes a readily available organic lard.

5 1/2 cups (680 grams) all-purpose flour or 5 cups (680 grams) bread flour

1 1/2 cups (360 grams) lukewarm water

1 1/2 tablespoons (14 grams) instant yeast

3 tablespoons (39 grams) lard

1 1/2 tablespoons barley malt syrup

1 1/2 teaspoons fine sea salt

Line a large baking sheet with parchment paper. In the bowl of a stand mixer, combine the flour, water, instant yeast, lard, barley malt and fine sea salt. Using the dough hook attachment, knead on low to medium speed for 9 to 12 minutes.

Turn the dough out onto the counter and shape it into 2 long, slim logs. Coil the logs together to form 2 spiral-shaped bread rolls. Put them on the prepared baking sheet, cover with another sheet of parchment paper and let the rolls double in size. This should take about 45 to 50 minutes, and ultimately measure about 9 inches in diameter.

When the dough has risen, heat the oven to 450°F. Bake rolls for 20 to 25 minutes, until golden brown.

CHEF'S NOTE: Barley malt adds both flavor and a boost for those yeasts working hard in your bread. You can also substitute molasses or sorghum syrup.

GNOCCO FRITTO

(FRIED DOUGH)

YIELDS about 10 small fried breads

When summer came to the little town of San Pietro, the smell of gnocco fritto—or crescentina, as some in Bologna call it—would fill the air. These flat rounds of fried dough were a favorite at numerous food festivals that pop up on summer nights in the towns around Bologna. Sagra del Tortellino (the festival of stuffed pasta), Sagra della Lepre (the festival of hare), Sagra dell'Asparagus (the asparagus festival)—the themes would vary, but almost always you'd find gnocco fritto on the menu, often stuffed with good prosciutto di Parma.

This recipe is similar to the biove bread, but with milk added for moisture to keep it soft while it fries. At Papavero, we cut gnocco fritto into squares so it fits into the bread basket, and we've turned it into a popular snack during aperitivo hour. People love them so much, they sometimes order two.

2 cups (250 grams) all-purpose flour

1 tablespoon plus 3/4 teaspoon (12 grams) instant yeast

Scant 2 teaspoons (9 grams) fine sea salt

1 tablespoon plus 3/4 teaspoon (16 grams) lard

1/4 cup (61 grams) lukewarm milk

1/2 cup water (120 grams), approximately

Lard, canola oil or peanut oil, for frying

Place flour, yeast, sea salt, lard, milk and water into the bowl of a stand mixer and knead with the hook attachment for about 10 minutes. Cover the bowl and let the dough double in size, about 1 hour.

Once the dough has doubled, sprinkle some flour on a countertop and turn the dough out onto it. With the aid of a rolling pin, roll out the dough into an even layer about 1/3-inch thick. (This takes some patience; you need to roll it pretty thin!) Cut into diamond shapes about 4 inches per side using a pasta cutter or a pizza cutter.

Fill a pot with a few inches of lard or oil and heat it to 325°F (a deep-fry thermometer will help with this). Working in batches, fry the bread, flipping to puff evenly on both sides. Remove from the oil when golden brown and place on a paper towel-lined plate. Pat dry, sprinkle with salt to taste and serve.

BECHAMEL SAUCE

YIELDS 8 cups

As noted in the lasagna recipe, bechamel sauce came to Bologna through the French—before that, lasagna was made without it. Since then, it's been used for pasta dishes, as well as with fall vegetables like fennel and cauliflower.

If you don't need 8 full cups of bechamel, simply use the ratio, which doesn't change. Butter and flour are always one to one, mixed with 8 to 10 parts milk. If you're making this for lasagna, wait until the sauce cools down a little bit. The texture will thicken as it cools.

1 cup (2 sticks/16 tablespoons) unsalted butter

1 cup all-purpose flour

A pinch of salt

A pinch of black pepper

A pinch of ground nutmeg

8 cups milk

Melt butter in a saucepan over medium heat, then add the flour and whisk until combined. Add the salt, pepper and nutmeg. Keep whisking over medium heat for about 2 minutes, or until the flour starts getting slightly more brown. Add the milk gradually to the pan while whisking (this should prevent lumps from forming). Cook for a couple of minutes, and when it's warm it's ready. You're looking for a sauce that's pourable, not sludgy but not runny either, thick enough to coat the back of a spoon.

RAGOUT ALLA BOLOGNESE

(BOLOGNESE SAUCE)

YIELDS roughly 8 cups

In the nineteenth century, most people started making Bolognese in the same way, using beef and pork or, in noble families, veal. It was more tomatoey then, to stretch the meat. At Papavero, we make it with about 70% meat and 30% tomato.

If you want to add veal, feel free, and we don't shy away from putting in leftover prosciutto, pancetta or scraps of mortadella. Grind them along with the rest of the meat.

1 onion, medium-sized

1 carrot, small

1 celery stalk

1/2 cup extra-virgin olive oil

1 pound ground pork, preferably pork shoulder

1 pound ground beef, preferably 80/20

1/2 cup dry red wine

1 14.5-ounce can peeled and crushed tomatoes

1/2 cup milk

Salt and pepper, to taste

Finely mince the onion, carrot and celery—use a knife or cut into large chunks and pulse in a food processor (this is called a soffritto).

In a large saucepan, add the olive oil, then add the soffritto vegetables. Turn the heat to medium-low and sauté on gentle heat. If the veggies start turning brown, add a bit of salt and water to the pan to prevent further browning. After about 5 minutes, once the vegetables are soft, add the ground meats to the pan and stir.

Cook on medium heat. When the meat has turned brown, add salt to taste. After a few minutes, add the wine to the pan and wait for the alcohol to evaporate, then add the crushed tomatoes.

Cook on low heat, uncovered, for approximately 3 to 3 1/2 hours. You should see some of the orangey meat fat eventually come to the surface of the sauce—that's a good sign! It means the meat is cooked. Add the milk, stir to emulsify a bit, and let cook for an additional 30 minutes. Season with salt and pepper to taste.

Let the Bolognese cool overnight. The next day, skim the fat from the top. To use in a lasagna, add about a cup of water to loosen. Otherwise, serve Bolognese with cooked pasta.

LASAGNE ALLA BOLOGNESE

(BOLOGNESE-STYLE LASAGNA)

YIELDS one 13-by-9-inch baking pan, about 12 portions

The Bolognese people have the French to thank for this style of lasagna. Napoleon Bonaparte's army introduced bechamel sauce to the beloved baked pasta during the years they occupied the Pope's territory of Emilia-Romagna in the 19th century.

The spinach that makes the lasagna sheets green also adds flavor. Italian specialty stores, including Fraboni's in Madison, often stock green pasta. Otherwise look for an imported dried pasta brand like De Cecco or Rustichella. Do not boil the noodles before using.

If I have done anything good for my kids, I have at least given them an appreciation for true lasagne alla Bolognese. Even now when we're at home, they ask me to make it for them. (Then again, my customers do the same!)

6 cups Bolognese ragout (page 24), **plus 1 cup water**

1 1/2 pounds dried green lasagna sheets (such as Granoro)

6 cups bechamel sauce (page 23), **plus 1 cup water**

2 1/4 cups (270 grams) grated Parmigiano-Reggiano

Preheat the oven to 400°F. In a 13-by-9-inch baking pan, spread a bit of ragout at the bottom. This will prevent your lasagna from sticking to the pan. Add a layer of pasta sheets, not necessarily overlapping them, but trying to make them fit the size of the pan.

Next, add another thin layer of ragout to the pan, followed by a layer of bechamel and a sprinkle of Parmigiano. Top with another layer of lasagna sheets. Continue until all the ingredients are utilized, ending with ragout, bechamel and cheese. You're looking to get four or five layers.

Cover the lasagna with foil and bake for 30 minutes. Then remove the foil and bake 30 minutes more, or until the top is browned and bubbly. Serve hot.

CHEF'S NOTE: Both the ragout and bechamel should be a bit loose. Dried lasagna sheets tend to absorb moisture very quickly during the baking process, and you don't want to eat a dried-out lasagna!

MEAT TORTELLI

(STUFFED MEAT PASTA)

YIELDS about 5 portions

This stuffed pasta can be found in many households in Bologna during the holidays, which doesn't mean you can't make it all year long. A typical accompaniment would be a good homemade broth, but "not-so-purists" also like tortelli with a good Bolognese ragout. We might serve it topped with browned butter and sage (as shown here), or with sautéed wild mushrooms.

Traditionally, the filling for tortellini was made by combining cooked meats and salumi scraps. If you don't happen to have pork loin on hand, consider using whatever leftover meat you have around (say, some chicken you used to make soup or stock).

FOR THE PASTA DOUGH:

2 1/3 cup (300 grams) all-purpose flour

3 whole eggs

FOR THE FILLING:

1/3 cup (2 ounces) Italian mortadella

Scant 1/2 cup (2 ounces) leftover cooked pork loin or veal

1/2 cup (1 ounce) prosciutto

3 tablespoons (1 ounce) Parmigiano-Reggiano cheese

2 eggs, divided

A pinch of nutmeg

Kosher salt

Pepper

To make the pasta dough, mix flour and three eggs on a counter. Knead together until all the flour is hydrated and the dough looks smooth, about 3 minutes. Cover the dough with plastic wrap and set aside for 20 to 30 minutes before using.

Get your meat ready for the filling by pulsing the mortadella, pork loin and prosciutto in a food processor. When the meat looks minced, add the Parmigiano, one egg, nutmeg, salt and pepper. Pulse to incorporate.

In a glass measuring cup, whisk the remaining egg, and get ready to assemble the tortelli. First, roll the pasta dough with an electric or hand-crank pasta machine until you can almost see through it. Using a pasta cutter, cut the dough into 3-inch squares. Dab two sides of each pasta square with a bit of whisked egg. Put a small amount of filling in the center of the square and fold over to create a triangle. Now, take the far ends of the triangle-shaped tortellino and pinch them together to seal. (See photos at right.)

When ready to serve, bring a pot of salted water to a boil. Cook the pasta in batches for 4 to 5 minutes. The pasta should be consumed the same day, but it can also be frozen, covered with plastic wrap, on a baking tray that has been dusted with flour for about a week.

CHEF'S NOTE: This recipe works for tortellini, tortelloni and tortellaci. The size will vary but the method is the same.

FINOCCHI GRATINATI

(FENNEL GRATIN)

YIELDS 4 generous portions

Fennel is a funny-looking vegetable, and I have discovered over the years that most Americans don't know what to do with it. But cooked properly and coated with a nice layer of creamy bechamel and good Parmigiano, fennel can be sublime.

You can use this preparation with cauliflower as well. Note that it's very rich—for some, it's enough for a main course.

1 pound fennel, or 3 to 4 small bulbs, trimmed

2 cups bechamel sauce (page 23)

1 cup (120 grams) grated Parmigiano-Reggiano cheese

CHEF'S NOTE: Use the leftover fennel scraps! Combine with a few slivers of garlic, dried bay leaves, fennel seeds and a sprinkle of salt, cover with foil and roast at 450°F for 45 minutes. Discard the bay leaves, then blend for a delicious fennel purée that you can use with a piece of roasted fish, roasted spring vegetables or to fill pasta (drain a bit first).

Bring a pot of salted water to a boil. Prepare a large bowl of ice water, and line a tray with paper towels. Cut the fennel bulbs into quarters, or eighths if large. Drop the fennel into the boiling water and cook until tender, about 5 to 6 minutes. Shock the fennel in the ice water, drain in a colander and dry on paper towels.

Preheat your oven to 450°F. Butter a baking pan (we use 6 1/2-by-4 1/2-inch) and spread a layer of bechamel on the bottom. Lay down your cooked fennel bulb slices without overlapping. Top with the bechamel, then the grated Parmigiano cheese. Bake until bubbly on top, about 25 to 28 minutes. Serve warm.

GNOCCHI DI PATATE

(POTATO DUMPLINGS)

YIELDS roughly 8 portions

At Papavero, we create different types of gnocchi depending on the season. The word "gnocchi" means "dumpling" in Italian and does not reference potatoes only, so we might make gnudi (ricotta-spinach gnocchi from Tuscany), pumpkin gnocchi from the Veneto region or bread gnocchi, known as "knodels" in German, found in the restaurants of the Trentino region.

The best kitchen-counter materials to work gnocchi dough are marble and wood. Metal counters tend to make the dough stick if there is not enough flour.

2 pounds creamy yellow potatoes such as Yukon Golds, peeled and cubed

Semolina flour, for dusting

1 1/3 cup (170 grams) all-purpose flour

2 whole eggs, whisked lightly

A pinch of salt

Add the potatoes to a pot of salted water and bring to a boil. Cook 10 to 12 minutes, until tender. Drain the potatoes in a colander and immediately put through a potato ricer. (If you do not have a ricer, a grater will also work.) Let the potatoes cool for 10 to 15 minutes.

Lightly dust a counter surface with semolina flour. Put the potatoes on the counter, then add the flour, eggs and a pinch of salt. Gently knead the flour into the eggs, using four to five quick motions. The goal is to obtain a smooth dough without overworking the potatoes, which otherwise could turn gluey.

Once all the ingredients are well incorporated, cut the dough into four parts with a bench scraper. Roll one piece at a time with your hands in an outward motion to form a string of dough about 1/2 to 3/4 inch in diameter.

Again using the bench scraper, cut the gnocchi into 1-inch segments. Store the gnocchi on a floured baking pan until ready to use. Gnocchi are best when used the same day, but if using the following day, cover them with a floured cotton towel to prevent oxidation, which may occur overnight. (Unfortunately it doesn't work well to freeze them.)

To cook the gnocchi, bring a large pot of salted water to a boil. Working in batches, drop in a few gnocchi. When they float, they're ready, usually about 1 minute. Remove to a plate and drain.

GNOCCHETTI DI PATATE CON RADICCHIO, ACETO BALSAMICO E SPECK

(POTATO DUMPLINGS WITH RADICCHIO, BALSAMIC VINEGAR AND SPECK)

YIELDS 8 portions

This recipe for gnocchetti (little gnocchi, made from potatoes) overlaps the Modena province and Bologna, in the Emilia-Romagna region of Italy. Papavero has been using this recipe for more than a decade, and it's similar to what you might find in an osteria in Bologna.

Sourcing is key for this simple recipe. Speck is a brined, aged smoked prosciutto that hails from the northern region of Trentino, and its smoky flavor is important here. If you can't find it, look for smoked meat, like smoked prosciutto or smoked ham.

Radicchio in its multiple variations (di Castelfranco, tardivo, Rosso, di Chioggia, di Verona) is the pride of many municipalities of the Veneto region. Traditional balsamic vinegar is the product of only two cities in Emilia-Romagna: Reggio Emilia and Modena. If you buy the really good stuff (like Villa Manodori), you can use even less than what's called for here.

1 1/2 cups chopped speck, smoked prosciutto or smoked ham

2 tablespoons extra-virgin olive oil

1 teaspoon (1 small clove) minced garlic

6 cups (8.5 ounces) chopped radicchio

1/8 to 1/4 cup good aged balsamic vinegar (see note)

2 1/2 cups (1 pound) potato gnocchi (store bought, or see recipe on page 32)

1 cup (4.25 ounces) grated Parmigiano cheese

Kosher salt, to taste

In a large pan, sauté the speck in olive oil until slightly translucent, then swiftly add the garlic and stir, taking care not to burn it. Add the radicchio to the pan next, along with salt for seasoning (be careful—speck tends to get salty when cooked).

Add a tablespoon of balsamic vinegar to deglaze the pan. Let the vinegar smell subside and the radicchio cook until slightly wilted, just a few minutes. Add the cooked gnocchi to the pan and stir together before turning off the heat.

Taste and adjust for salt and acidity. Top with Parmigiano and serve.

CHEF'S NOTE: Beware of imitation balsamico. The real stuff has a red label around the neck of the bottle that certifies the traditional method used in making this delicious product. Stay away from aceti (vinegar) made with preservatives or sweetened with caramel.

Photo credit: Ruthie Hauge, Cap Times

PARMIGIANA DI MELANZANE

(EGGPLANT PARMESAN)

YIELDS one 13-by-9-inch pan, about 8 portions

Growing up, my maternal grandparents lived about half an hour away, and I have fond memories of Sunday lunches at their home. My grandma would often cook recipes she'd learned from the family of my grandfather while the two were dating during World War II.

This classic eggplant dish has been a hit at Papavero, especially in the summer, and I do not recommend eating it bubbling hot. It's typical in Sicily and the remainder of the southern part of Italy, especially during the hottest days of summer, to eat dishes like this (or caponata) at room temperature or even cold.

2 pounds eggplant, 3 to 4 medium-sized

Canola oil for frying

Salt and pepper, to taste

Glug of olive oil

1 clove (1 teaspoon) garlic, smashed

3 cups (726 grams) canned crushed tomatoes

A sprig of fresh basil

Kosher salt

1 1/2 cup (170 grams) grated unaged provolone cheese

1 1/2 cup (113 grams) grated Parmigiano cheese

Slice the eggplants lengthwise about 1 inch thick. Prepare a plate or pan lined with absorbent paper towels. Heat canola oil to 325°F degrees (a deep fry thermometer is useful here). Fry eggplant in batches until lightly browned. Drain the eggplant on paper towels, patting both sides to remove excess oil. Season the eggplants with salt and pepper.

Prepare the tomato sauce. To a saucepan, add a glug of olive oil, the smashed garlic, tomatoes, basil and a pinch of salt. Over medium heat, bring to a bare simmer, and cook gently for 20 to 25 minutes. You want enough for several layers, so don't reduce it too much. Remove the sauce from the heat. Discard the garlic and basil. Taste to adjust for salt, then put the sauce in a fine mesh strainer set over a bowl and let drain for about 5 minutes. Allow to cool down and discard the liquid.

Into a 13-by-9 inch baking dish with raised edges, spoon a bit of the tomato sauce first, then lay the fried eggplants without overlapping, trying to cover as much of the tomato sauce as you can. Add more tomato sauce, then some provolone. Proceed the same way for the next layers, finishing up with the grated Parmigiano.

Bake at 450°F for about 20 minutes or until the cheese is melted. Serve warm but not hot.

CRESPELLE

(ITALIAN CREPE)

YIELDS 8 to 10 portions

Ah, crespelle! The bane of every prep cook at Papavero. Over the years, it has become almost an initiation rite to have the new cooks learn how to make crespelle, or Italian crepes, at the restaurant. Stuffed in many different savory ways (plus a sweet chocolate cream filling as a dessert), this dish has come on and off the Papavero dinner menu at least as many times as the years we've been open. It's a local favorite.

If you travel around Italy, you'll encounter different crespelle fillings in different regions. In Florence, crespelle are stuffed with ricotta and spinach, then smothered with bechamel and tomato sauce. At Papavero, a classic spring crespella is stuffed with asparagus, Parmigiano and ricotta, then covered in bechamel and sautéed wild mushrooms before going in the oven.

A nonstick pan is essential for this recipe, otherwise the crepe is likely to stick. The restaurant recipe works with a scale, but we've provided volume measurements if you prefer them. Again, this recipe is quite heavy! Scale it down as necessary.

FOR THE CREPE:

4 3/4 cups (592 grams) all-purpose flour

3/4 cup plus 2 tablespoons (213 grams) whole milk

4 eggs

A pinch of salt

Ghee or clarified butter, for cooking the crepes (see note)

FOR THE FILLING:

Scant 2 cups (340 grams) blanched or wilted spinach

2 3/4 cup (650 grams) fresh ricotta cheese

Scant 2 cups (240 grams) grated Parmigiano cheese

1/2 teaspoon ground nutmeg

Salt and pepper

4 cups of bechamel (page 23)**, thinned slightly with water**

Grana Padano, for sprinkling (optional)

To make the crepe, whisk together the flour, milk, eggs and pinch of salt. Let the batter sit for 10 to 15 minutes.

Heat an 8-inch pan nonstick pan over medium heat. Drop in a bit of melted ghee or butter, then pour enough batter to cover the bottom of the pan, swirling the batter around.

Once the crepe is done on one side, use a heat-resistant spatula to flip the crepe to the other side, and let it warm up for just a few seconds. This is just to ensure that the crepe won't stay too wet on that side.

Set the cooked crepe aside. Proceed the same way with the rest of the batter until done, layering parchment or wax paper between the crepes so they don't stick together.

To make the filling, first make sure your spinach is well dried and drained from all excessive water. Chop it roughly, then mix it in a large bowl with the ricotta cheese, Parmigiano cheese and nutmeg. Adjust the seasoning with salt and pepper.

To assemble, heat your oven to 500°F. Place several spoonfuls (1/3 cup) of filling into each crepe, leaving about an inch around. Fold two opposing sides toward the center, then tuck in a third side, like you're making a little burrito. Roll toward the fourth side to make a little bundle.

Ladle a small amount of bechamel on the bottom of individual small baking dishes or one 13-by-9-inch pan. Place crespelle (two per small plate, if using) on the bechamel, and ladle more sauce on top of them. Sprinkle with Grana Padano cheese, if using. Bake 10 to 12 minutes, or until nice and bubbly and slightly browned on top.

CHEF'S NOTE: Organic Valley makes a shelf-stable ghee, or make your own by melting butter in the microwave in a large container, then letting it cool and separate. The clear fat is what you want.

SALAME DI CIOCCOLATO

(CHOCOLATE ROLL)

YIELDS 2 chocolate rolls

Salame di cioccolato is a ubiquitous dessert in the central part of Italy. Regional variations adjust the type of liquor used, or the (healthy!) amount of butter utilized in the recipe.

If your butter is very cold, let it soften for 20 minutes on the counter to make it easier to work with. Use a scale for the best results. Without the right ratios of ingredients, even a simple dessert like this one can turn into a disaster. There are raw eggs in this, but the risk of illness is very low.

1/2 cup (85 grams) bittersweet chocolate (discs, like pistoles or wafers)

5-10 small shortbread or butter cookies (85 grams), such as Leibniz or Balocco

1/2 cup (56 grams) whole almonds, toasted

8 tablespoons (113 grams) unsalted butter (Papavero uses high fat, European style)

2/3 cup (131 grams) granulated sugar

2 whole eggs

2/3 cup (57 grams) good quality cocoa powder, such as Valrhona

3 tablespoons (30 grams) dark rum (see note)

1 tablespoon (10 grams) Marsala wine

1 pinch of kosher salt

Drop or two of vanilla extract (optional)

Using a double boiler or a microwave, melt the chocolate. Let cool slightly.

In a food processor, add the cookies and almonds and pulse three times until very roughly chopped. (You can also crush and chop these, respectively—you want them uneven, so it looks rustic).

In the bowl of a stand mixer, mix the butter and sugar until creamy and light yellow. Add the eggs and the cocoa powder and mix just to incorporate. Scrape the sides of the bowl. Add the rum, the Marsala wine, kosher salt and the melted chocolate to the bowl. Mix just until combined; it's OK if the mixture is a little rough. Fold in the crumbled cookies and the nuts. It should look like cookie dough. Taste, and if it seems to need a drop or two of vanilla, add that now.

Put a layer of plastic wrap on your counter and transfer the dough to it. Roll the dough like a sausage, making two rolls each roughly 6 inches long and about 1 3/4 inch in diameter. Secure the ends with pieces of string. Chill for at least 3 hours, then slice and serve.

Serve with a scoop of ice cream, a dollop of whipped cream, a chocolate grappa from Italy or a combination of these.

CHEF'S NOTE: You can make this without alcohol, just add a teaspoon or so of vanilla for aroma.

ZUPPA INGLESE

(ITALIAN-STYLE ENGLISH TRIFLE)

YIELDS about 10 portions

Growing up, zuppa Inglese was not one of my favorite desserts. Versions often found in Bologna restaurants can be boozy, and for a kid the Campari is a little bitter. I like it much better now. During one of my trips home as an adult, I went to a restaurant with a long list of desserts and I chose this one. Ladyfingers are very absorbent, so if you decide to substitute another cookie, keep that in mind.

FOR THE SYRUP:

1 cup sugar

1 cup water

2/3 cup Campari or Alkermes liqueur (see note)

FOR THE CUSTARDS:

8 eggs

3/4 plus 2 tablespoons (6 ounces) granulated white sugar

1/2 cup (2 ounces) flour

2 3/4 cup (24 ounces) whole milk

1 lemon peel (peel from a whole lemon), cut into strips

1 cinnamon stick

Generous pinch of salt

1 cup (3 ounces) cocoa powder (plus more for serving) or 2/3 cup bittersweet chocolate, melted

1 dozen (4 ounces) ladyfingers cookies

Mix the sugar, water and Campari in a little pot, place on the stove and bring to a simmer over medium heat to dissolve the sugar. Set aside and cool down.

Next, prepare the custards. Combine the eggs and sugar together in the bowl of a stand mixer. Whisk in the flour thoroughly, being careful to remove as many lumps as you can. In a saucepan on the stove, scald the milk (bring to a boil, then remove from heat). Add lemon peel and cinnamon stick to the milk to steep. After 5 minutes, remove them.

Add the scalded milk to the bowl with the eggs and sugar and mix on low speed using the paddle attachment. Return this custard base to a heavy-bottomed pan on the stovetop and whisk over medium-low heat until it thickens up. This can take 8 to 10 minutes on a low simmer, and you're looking for the custard to thicken. Strain the custard if there are still lumps from the flour, or if you like a very silky texture.

Season to taste with a generous pinch of salt.

Split the custard into two equal parts. To one half, add cocoa powder or melted bittersweet chocolate (such as Valrhona). Set the custard aside and let it cool to room temperature.

Assemble the dessert in a clear-sided serving dish, bowl, Pyrex pan or individual dishes. Add a layer of chocolate custard to the bottom. Dip the ladyfingers cookies briefly in the Campari mixture. Add a layer of the dipped cookies, then a layer of yellow custard. Refrigerate until set, at least 4 hours (overnight is great). Serve with a sprinkle of cocoa powder on the top.

CHEF'S NOTE: Use leftover Campari syrup in cocktails or spritzes. Vary this recipe with fresh raspberries or strawberries in summer.

ZUCCHINE RIPIENE

(STUFFED ZUCCHINI)

YIELDS about 5 to 6 generous portions

This is another Tuscan recipe from my Grandma Iris, my mother's mom. She is from Pistoia, a small city near Florence. Her mother had an osteria, and she was cooking all the time. She learned some Sicilian dishes from her husband's mom, but the rest of her repertoire was all from Tuscany—stuffed peppers, baked tomatoes with breadcrumbs, roasted dishes, Parmigiana and rabbit.

For stuffed zucchini, all you need is some good zucchini from the farmers' market or the garden, a little ricotta and Parmigiano, and salumi (mortadella, if you can find it). It's great at room temperature. Even the kids will like it!

5 whole green zucchini (about 2 pounds), sliced in half lengthwise and seeded

1 1/2 cups (about 16 ounces) fresh whole milk ricotta cheese (see note)

1/2 cup (2 ounces) Parmigiano-Reggiano, grated

A pinch of nutmeg

1 tablespoon chopped parsley

1 egg

1/3 cup (about 2 ounces) finely diced mortadella or other salumi scraps

3 tablespoons plain breadcrumbs

Salt and pepper, to taste

Preheat your oven to 450°F. Blanch the zucchini by bringing a pot of salted water to a boil, then dropping in the halved zucchini and simmering for about 5 minutes. Transfer the zucchini to a bowl of iced water, drain and pat dry.

Line a baking tray with parchment paper and place the zucchini on it, cut side up. Season with salt and pepper. Combine the ricotta, Parmigiano, nutmeg, parsley, egg and mortadella in a mixing bowl.

Stuff the zucchini with the mixture. Level off, then top with breadcrumbs. Bake for about 18 to 20 minutes, or until light brown, and serve.

CHEF'S NOTE: If your ricotta is very wet, place it on a few layers of paper towels and let it drain for 5 to 10 minutes.

Photo credit: Shutterstock

LA MONTAGNA

THE MOUNTAINS (THE DOLOMITES)

The Dolomites are part of the vast arc of the Italian alps, stretching for thousands of miles west to east, separating the Trento and Friuli regions of Italy from France, Switzerland, Austria and Slovenia. The largest part of these mountains divides the Trentino region from neighboring Austria. The German language is spoken on both sides of the Alps, and Tyrolean culture is part of both physical regions.

Nothing here could be more different from the Tuscan coast, which is probably why my family loved it. I'm very fond of days camping in those mountains.

A typical day of camping would start with a run to the local bakery to procure some bread for the day. My Aunt Laura, the organizer, would turn delicious, fragrant buns into sandwiches for our "al sacco" lunch (literally, "al sacco" means "to bag," and refers to a packed lunch). Those sandwiches often included cold cuts, sometimes smoked meats like speck and stinky cheese like Raschera, Toma and Dobbiaco.

Every other day we'd set off on a hike to reach a certain peak, then eat somewhere nearby at a local "rifugio." Rifugi are little huts or houses where hikers can stop for a rest, get a little food and grappa, or simply respite from a fast and furious summer shower. On the menu at these unpretentious little trattorie would be classics like as polenta **(page 57)** with braised capriolo (a small local deer), gnocchi **(page 32)** with porcini mushrooms or sage and butter, and goulash **(page 52)**. Dessert might be a fresh ricotta bavarese (a creamy molded dessert) with wild berries, a sachertorte or apple strudel. (All of these dishes would eventually take their place on the Osteria Papavero menu.)

As we hiked in the woods, my uncle would look around for wild mushrooms, especially the renowned porcini or king bolete. In August, my aunt would search for wild blackberries and blueberries. On rest days, we might venture inside the little town where we were camping, shop at the local stores and possibly eat at a local "stube," or restaurant.

As my uncles got a little too old to camp and I became a teenager, we swapped tents for residences. Residences are Alpine-looking houses available during summer season for rent. Now, instead of being forced to sun dry our foraged mushrooms, my uncle would have a stove available. This allowed him to turn out delicious mushroom soups **(page 48)** and sauces, while my aunt prepared blackberry tarts.

This section could easily appear in a German cookbook. Polenta and goulash appear in German-speaking regions of Tyrol, and are not necessarily Italian. Bomboloni have a German name and are called "krapfen" in Tyrol and Austria. Canederli (or knodels) could be cooked by a German ex-pat living in Madison. And again, this is heavier food because of that culture in the mountains. These dishes translate well to fall and winter in Wisconsin.

ZUPPA DI FUNGHI

(WILD MUSHROOM STEW)

YIELDS about 6 cups

Many years ago, I was eating at a little place on the Tuscan hills of Pisa when I had this stew of wild mushrooms. It tasted nothing like typical canned cream of mushroom soup. Earthy, rustic and redolent of the smell of the woods, this stew was an utter surprise. Knowing the bounty of Wisconsin mushrooms—I became a forager a few years later—I knew this could easily be reproduced in Madison.

1 cup (1 ounce) dried porcini mushrooms

2 cups hot water

2 to 3 cloves (1 tablespoon) chopped garlic

1 cup mixed soft herbs, such as dill, tarragon, parsley and oregano, picked and roughly chopped, divided

2/3 cup extra-virgin olive oil

2 cups (1 pound) assorted wild mushrooms, such as shiitake, oyster or porcini, cut into bite-sized pieces

Salt, to taste

1/2 cup dry white wine

2 cups (17 ounces) crushed canned tomatoes

3 tablespoons grated Parmigiano-Reggiano

Toasted country-style bread (optional)

Break the dried mushrooms into pieces and pour the hot water over them to reconstitute. Set this aside to steep for 15 minutes. Meanwhile, in a large Dutch oven or stew pot set over medium-low heat, sauté the garlic and half of the herbs with the olive oil.

Working in batches if necessary so the mushrooms do not steam, add the wild mushrooms to the pot, season with salt and stir, nudging the heat up to medium. After the mushrooms begin to reduce in size, add the wine to the pot. When the smell of alcohol has subsided, add the tomatoes, chopped dried mushrooms and reserved porcini water (strain if there's grit on the bottom).

Turn down the heat and let cook for about 20 minutes, or until the mushrooms are tender but not mushy. Serve the stew warm and topped with cheese and the remainder of the chopped soft herbs, along with country-style bread if desired.

CANEDERLI

(BREAD DUMPLINGS)

YIELDS about 20 canederli

A few fresh sage leaves, for serving They only make these dumplings (also called knodels in German) in a couple regions in northern Italy. The concept is simply using leftovers, or scraps, to make something valuable. Sometimes they mix in meat, scraps of salumi or speck. If you have leftover greens, like spinach or chard, you can blanch them, squeeze them and chop them well before adding to this recipe.

Canederli come in two ways: in broth—the same as tortellini in broth—or with brown butter and sage. Sometimes you find little variations like poppy seeds. And always there's grated Alpine cheese—like gruyere, but funkier. One tester who worked on this recipe described them "like Thanksgiving stuffing meets matzo ball."

7 cups (10 ounces) stale bread

3 cups (24 ounces) milk

3 cups (24 ounces) water, more if necessary

1 medium onion, diced

2 scallions, diced

1 small clove (1/2 teaspoon) garlic, minced

A pinch of ground nutmeg

A few celery leaves, finely chopped

1 cup (3.5 ounces) Parmigiano or other northern Italian-style aged cheese, grated, plus more for garnish

4 eggs

1/2 cup (2 ounces) plain breadcrumbs

2/3 cup (3 ounces) all-purpose flour

Melted butter, for serving

Fresh sage, for serving

NOTE that this is a two-day dish. Chilling the dough balls overnight makes the dumplings less likely to fall apart in the water when they cook.

In a large bowl, soak the stale bread in milk and water for about 15 minutes. It can help to use a piece of parchment paper to push the bread down in the liquid and cover the bread. After soaking, squeeze all the moisture out, laying the bread on a sheet tray lined with paper towels.

In another large bowl, mix the bread with the rest of the ingredients. If the mix still looks fairly wet, let it rest for a good half hour on more paper towels. Shape the dough into balls with a diameter of about 2 inches. Place these in the refrigerator and let rest overnight.

When it's time to cook, bring some salted water to a boil. Cook dumplings a few at a time for 2 to 3 minutes until they start floating (or at least are no longer sinking). Remove the dumplings with a slotted spoon. Serve with melted butter and fresh sage leaves, topped with grated cheese.

GOULASCH

(GOULASH)

YIELDS about 4 quarts (serves about 10)

Cooks from Hungary or Austria, Slovenia and Italy will all say that the "original" goulash recipe comes from the place where they were born. The truth is, they are all right! Recipes for goulash tend to vary in seasoning and sides (pasta, noodles, rice, polenta). This version is one I often had in Trentino, in the southern Tyrol region of Italy at the border to the Austrian Alps.

The meat will taste stringy if you don't add enough fat at the beginning and maintain the level of liquid during cooking. This makes a large batch, but if you're making goulash for four, you might as well make it for eight. It scales well, freezes well, and tastes better the day after you make it.

Olive oil

4 pounds of boneless beef shoulder (or top round/ boneless short ribs), cut into 2-to-3-inch cubes

8 cups (2 pounds) of peeled yellow onions, sliced horizontally about 1 inch thick

3 tablespoons sweet paprika (make some of this hot paprika if you like)

1 tablespoon whole caraway seeds

2 whole dried bay leaves

2 tablespoons dried marjoram

1 bottle (750 mL) red wine

1 3/4 cups (1 pound) canned crushed tomatoes (not fire-roasted)

Salt and pepper, to taste

Butter (optional)

In a large braising pan, heat a tablespoon or two of olive oil and sear the beef cubes until browned, working in batches so as not to overcrowd the pan. Remove the beef to a plate.

Add the onions to the pan. At this stage you can add some butter or use more olive oil. Add the paprika, caraway seeds, bay leaves and marjoram, and cook until the onion is barely translucent but not mushy. (Add a little water if necessary to keep the onion from browning.) Return the seared beef to the pan, then add the wine and tomatoes.

Season with salt and pepper, cover the pan, lower the heat and let the meat cook until tender. Check periodically to make sure the meat is barely submerged in liquid. Add water as necessary. Cook for 3 to 4 hours, until fork tender, depending on which cut of beef you chose. Adjust salt to taste.

We like to serve goulash with polenta (**page 57**), but it's delicious with buttered noodles, gnocchi, mashed cheesy potatoes and canederli (bread dumplings, **page 50**) as well.

BOMBOLONI
(FILLED DOUGHNUTS)

YIELDS 16 doughnuts

For a long time, bomboloni (or krapfen, "filled doughnuts" in German) was a recipe I didn't tackle because there was always something wrong with them. Sometimes they didn't rise. Sometimes there was too much sugar, or they'd get too brown. Sometimes they were dense. I would never run them at the restaurant, because there was always something that made them not come out.

Then I found this recipe in an insert in an Italian newspaper called "Cook" where they invite chefs to publish their best recipes. And it works! We use cake flour to make them fluffier. Here we use Nutella, but you can fill them with jam or pastry cream. Top with a sprinkle of powdered sugar.

1 3/4 cups plus 1 1/2 tablespoons (450 grams) cake flour or all-purpose flour

1 cup (227 grams) whole milk

6 tablespoons (71 grams) granulated sugar

5 tablespoons (71 grams) butter, softened

2 teaspoons (14 grams) fine sea salt

3 1/2 tablespoons (46 grams) instant yeast

1/2 teaspoon vanilla extract

1 egg plus 1 egg yolk

Zest of 1/2 orange, chopped

Neutral oil (canola, peanut or lard), for frying

1 cup (296 grams) Nutella, for filling

Powdered sugar, for sprinkling

Combine flour, milk, sugar, butter, salt, yeast, vanilla, egg, egg yolk and orange zest in the bowl of a stand mixer fitted with a dough hook. Knead for about 12 minutes. The dough should be neither too sticky nor too dry.

Prepare a baking sheet lined with parchment paper. Scrape the bowl, transfer the dough to a counter and cut the dough into 16 pieces (a scraper works well for this). Using slightly wet hands and a pinching motion, shape into balls about the size of a ping pong ball, and set with the "sealed" side down.

Transfer the bomboloni to the baking sheet, leaving 3 to 4 inches between each ball. Cover with another sheet of parchment paper and let the balls double in size. This should take between an hour and 90 minutes.

...continued next page

Prepare a tray lined with paper towels. Heat 3-4 inches of neutral oil in a very large frying pan. Keep the oil stable between 325–350°F. In small batches of 3 or 4, gently transfer the bomboloni to the pot. Brown them on one side. With a spider or slotted spoon, flip to brown on the other side. Remove from the oil at once and drain well on absorbent paper. Repeat with remaining doughnuts.

Cool for an hour at room temperature. Using a pastry bag with a decorating tip (like Ateco size 825, 7/16 inch), pipe Nutella into the middle of each doughnut. A paring knife can help if the filling is coming out the top—also, should this happen, use a smaller amount. Serve sprinkled with powdered sugar.

CHEF'S NOTE: The bomboloni can take close to 2 hours to rise. Make sure that the balls are in a warm part of the kitchen.

POLENTA

(ITALIAN-STYLE GRITS)

YIELDS about 6 to 7 portions

Polenta is an excellent accompaniment to dishes that are earthy and substantial—braised dishes like wild boar stew or braised beef, or really anything that is meaty and cheesy. In the north, they'll make a fondue of Alpine cheeses and pour the polenta on top. In Trentino, they serve polenta with cheese and mushrooms.

During service at Papavero, cooks set cooked polenta in a warm spot above the stove, covered with plastic wrap and aluminum foil, so it stays just soft enough to scoop.

4 cups water

1 1/2 cups (250 grams) dry polenta (coarse cornmeal)

2/3 cup (150 grams) butter, unsalted

1 cup (120 grams) Parmigiano-Reggiano

Salt and pepper, to taste

In a Dutch oven or saucepan (preferably not stainless steel), bring the water to a simmer, then add the dry cornmeal to the water, whisking constantly to prevent lumps. Cover the pan and let cook on low heat for about 15 to 20 minutes. The polenta should look fairly thick (if it's too thick for you, add water or milk). Remove the pan from the stove and add the butter, cheese and salt and pepper to taste. Whisk well, taste again and serve.

IL MARE

THE SEA—CASTIGLIONCELLO

If you like soccer, you may be familiar with the likes of Ronaldo and Messi. For me, the best memories of soccer go back to 1982. It was the peak of summer, and I was sitting on the couch of my maternal grandfather's vacation house in Castiglioncello (in the Livorno province).

My grandfather Vincenzo and I were waiting to see the Italian national team face the two soccer giants of the time, Brazil and Argentina. Despite all predictions, that Italian soccer team went on to win the world championship, making one chubby 10-year-old kid very happy.

Going to Castiglioncello meant going to the sea. Even though the eastern coast of Italy was considerably closer to my hometown in Bologna (about an hour and 15 minutes, driving), my grandfather had bought a vacation house many years ago in this small, beautiful town on the Tuscan "riviera." That's where my aunts spent their teenage years vacationing, and where two of them found the loves of their lives—my uncles, Enzo and Renzo.

At 10, I was much too young for romance, but those summers in Castiglioncello were always fun. On a typical day at the sea, my grandparents would take me to the closest beach, where I built sandcastles with my cousins and went swimming for several hours per day. We often brought food from home in packed lunches, but if we happened to still be at the beach during the afternoon, we might get a treat, either a "ghiacciolo" (popsicle) or a "schiacciatina" (a little round olive oil focaccia, often stuffed with cold cuts).

At night we'd have dinner with the rest of the family, either at my Aunt Laura's or my Aunt Carla's. My Uncle Enzo, Carla's husband, called me a "longobardo," meaning a butter-eating barbarian from the north of Italy. He was joking about the superiority of olive-growing Tuscany; I took no offense in that.

I didn't see anything better than eating "barbarian food" in Bologna all year long and then enjoying Tuscan fare all summer. We got pristine seafood from the Tyrrhenian Sea, sometimes caught by my uncles themselves (try my Uncle Renzo's stew of mussels, octopus and kale, **page 68**). There were always tasty Pecorino cheeses on hand, and earthy vegetable soups like ribollita **(page 64)** and pappa al pomodoro, made with tomatoes three ways **(page 71)**. I've included a recipe here for my Uncle Renzo's panzanella **(page 62)**. With bread that's soft, not toasted, I find it more refreshing than the crunchy style most Madison diners prefer.

In September, we'd start getting ready to travel back north and resume school—and I would already be fantasizing about the next time I could be back in Castiglioncello, on the sea.

FISH BRESAOLA

(CURED FISH)

YIELDS about 3 pounds

The first few years at Papavero we made salumi with meats, but we weren't doing anything with fish. I started looking into who was making salumi with fish on the coast, and with that inspiration combined with knowledge of gravlax and smoked salmon, we started experimenting. It worked right away.

Fish is seasonal. Call your local fish shop or fish counter for fresh swordfish, albacore tuna or blue marlin, all of which will work in this recipe. The ratio of fish to salt is important here. You cannot put a large fish in salt overnight and expect it to be cured.

Try cured fish on toast with aioli and arugula or some fresh farmer's cheese.

1/2 cup total of a mix of spices, such as bay leaves, cloves and black peppercorns

1/2 cup fresh herbs, such as rosemary, sage and thyme, roughly chopped

3 cups (1 1/2 pounds) coarse kosher salt

1 cup (1/2 pound) brown sugar

3 to 3 1/2 pounds swordfish loin (or opah, wahoo or albacore tuna)

In a dry skillet, toast spices gently until they are aromatic. Grind in a spice grinder. In a non-reactive tray large enough to hold the fish, mix the spices, herbs, salt and sugar. Put the fish loin in the tray and rub it all over with the salt and spice mixture. Cover well enough so that you don't see the surface of the fish. Cover the tray and refrigerate for 24 hours.

The next day, remove the fish from the salt, and rinse it off well under running water. The loin should feel relatively firm. Serve sliced thin, or cold smoke it for added flavor. Consume it within a week.

RENZO'S PANZANELLA

(ITALIAN BREAD SALAD)

YIELDS 5 portions

My Uncle Renzo lives in Tuscany, and I spent a lot of time with him during my summers there. There's never not panzanella at his house in the summer—he grows his own vegetables and has a wood-fired oven in his garden. He often goes fishing, so there are always herbs and tomatoes, as well as the fish that he catches. It's not a bad life in the summer.

We can't serve panzanella this way in the restaurant—people want the crisp, crunchy texture of fried bread. But this softer style is more traditional and gives you something cooling and refreshing. (To me, there's nothing cooling about a crispy piece of bread.) Use Tuscan sourdough or a similar bread with a nice crunch, and even soaked it will have good flavor.

If you don't like the taste of raw onions, slice them thinly and soak for 10 to 12 minutes in cold water to remove some of the acrid taste. Pat them dry and add them to the salad.

1 pound stale bread, preferably country-style, cut roughly into cubes

2 seedless cucumbers, sliced across into 1/2-inch rounds, lightly salted

3 heirloom tomatoes, cubed and lightly salted

1 large red onion, peeled and sliced across into 1/3-inch slices

1/3 cup red wine vinegar

1/2 cup extra-virgin olive oil

A dozen fresh basil leaves

Salt and pepper, to taste

1 cup good quality Italian canned tuna, well drained (optional)

Soak the bread in a bowl filled with cold water for about 10 to 12 minutes. Squeeze the water out with your hands and set the bread aside on a tray lined with paper towels.

In a bowl, combine the bread with the cucumbers, tomatoes, red onion, red wine vinegar, olive oil, basil leaves, salt and pepper. Add the tuna if using. Serve immediately.

INSALATA RIFATTA

(COLD STEAK SALAD)

YIELDS about 6 to 7 portions

"Rifatta" means "redone," or "done twice" in Italian. You could think of this recipe as a scraps salad, as the beef is usually leftover from another use. At Papavero we use smoked brisket because that's what diners prefer. Leftover beef roast works well too. It's a brilliant picnic dish.

This recipe is traditionally made with Calabrian chilies. If you can't find them, sambal oelek makes a nice substitute. For smoked brisket by the pound, look to local barbecue spots.

1 pound smoked brisket, thinly sliced

2 seedless cucumbers, sliced across into 1-inch thick rondelles

2 cups cherry tomatoes, sliced

8 cups (8 ounces) spring mix or other fresh lettuce

1 teaspoon fresh chopped chili or chili sauce, such as sambal oelek

4 tablespoons scallions, sliced across

1 spring each of fresh basil and mint

1 1/2 tablespoons balsamic vinegar

4 1/2 tablespoons extra-virgin olive oil

Salt and pepper, to taste

Combine all ingredients in a large bowl. Serve cold.

LA RIBOLLITA

(TUSCAN BREAD SOUP)

YIELDS about 8 cups

Ribollita, which means "reboil," is a soup that's very popular in Florence, in Tuscany. It belongs to both the city and the countryside, and it's one of the oldest soups recorded in Tuscan cookery books. It uses day-old bread, kale and cannellini beans, one of the cheapest beans to grow. I believe this comes from poverty.

I used to have ribollita in my uncle's house, and I love this soup because it's connected to my childhood. But even if I'd hated it, I wouldn't have been able to avoid it. Drive 50 minutes from Bologna and it's everywhere.

At Papavero, we use dried beans, soaked overnight and cooked in the morning, but here, canned are a good substitute. If your bread is very stale it can be hard to cut; cube it before it gets too hard.

5 tablespoons extra-virgin olive oil

1 medium onion, diced

1 carrot, sliced into half-inch rounds

1 sprig of basil

1 sprig of sage

1 15-ounce can cannellini beans, drained and rinsed

1 cup (8 ounces) canned crushed tomatoes

2 bunches (11 to 14 ounces) Tuscan kale

2 cups (3 ounces) stale, crusty bread, diced

Sea salt

Grated Parmigiano-Reggiano for garnish (optional)

Set a large soup pot over medium heat. Add the olive oil, onion, carrot and a sprig each of basil and sage. Sweat until translucent, about 5 to 10 minutes. Add the cannellini beans to the pot, then the tomatoes, and stir together. Add enough water to the pan to submerge your vegetables, about 1 1/2 cup. Season lightly with salt and bring to a simmer.

As the soup begins to cook, stem the kale, roughly chop the leaves and add the leaves to the pot. Stir the soup, then let cook on low heat for 15 to 20 minutes, or until the kale leaves are soft.

Add the stale bread to the pot and bring back to a simmer once again. Shut the burner off and let it sit. Taste and adjust salt.

Ribollita is better the following day. Reheat the soup and serve with grated Parmigiano on top, or without if you prefer it the Tuscan way.

PASTA ZUCCHINE E RICOTTA

(PASTA WITH ZUCCHINI, RICOTTA AND BASIL)

YIELDS about 6 to 7 portions

Longtime Papavero cook Alessandro Monachello likes to claim this pasta as his, but my Aunt Carla made this all the time in the summer with zucchini from her own garden. You could substitute other kinds of summer squash or eggplant, or even winter squash; just cook it a bit longer.

1 pound short pasta (like penne, fusilli, orecchiette or rigatoni)

1 to 2 tablespoons extra-virgin olive oil

5 medium zucchini, sliced into 1/2-inch rounds

3 cloves (1 tablespoon) garlic, minced

A pinch of hot pepper flakes

1/2 cup dry white wine

6 fresh basil leaves (or more, to taste)

1 1/2 cups (10 to 11 ounces) good quality ricotta cheese

1 cup pecorino cheese, grated

Cook pasta in boiling salted water until al dente (time will vary based on pasta type). Drain well.

In a large sauté pan, heat the olive oil until it smokes. Panfry the zucchini rounds in batches, taking care not to overcrowd the pan, until they appear lightly browned on both sides. Remove the zucchini onto a plate as they look ready and season them lightly with salt.

After removing the last zucchini, add the garlic and hot pepper flakes to the pan with a bit more olive oil and stir. Immediately add the white wine so the garlic does not burn, and let the alcohol evaporate.

Add the fresh basil to the pan, followed by the pasta and the ricotta. Remove the pan from the heat and stir just to combine. Serve the pasta topped with pecorino cheese.

ZIMINO DI COZZE, POLPO E CAVOLO NERO

(STEW OF BLACK MUSSELS, OCTOPUS AND TUSCAN KALE)

YIELDS about 8 portions

This is the second recipe in this book from my Uncle Renzo, who lives in a little town in Tuscany called Castiglioncello on the sea. Sometimes I omit the bread and add beans or chickpeas for people who are gluten free. Sometimes we omit the mussels. I have served it on our seafood platter as a stew—and as an appetizer, it works great.

You can use a food processor to speed up the chop on the soffritto (onion, celery and carrot). Note that mussels aren't the kind of thing that keep, so cut this recipe in half if you're not making it for a family gathering. Cooked chickpeas can be a nice addition to this zimino recipe. Add them after the wine.

1 to 2 tablespoons extra-virgin olive oil

1/2 cup onion, diced

1/4 cup celery, diced

1/4 cup carrot, diced

1 clove (1 teaspoon) garlic, minced

1 teaspoon hot pepper flakes

1/2 cup dried porcini mushrooms, rehydrated with 2 cups of hot water (optional)

1 pound cooked octopus tentacles, cut crosswise into bite-size pieces (see note)

1 sprig each of fresh basil and fresh sage

1 bunch (about 8 ounces) Tuscan kale leaves, stemmed and roughly chopped

Salt and pepper, to taste

2 cups dry red wine, such as cabernet or merlot

2 cups canned crushed tomatoes

2 cups seafood stock or clam juice

8 ounces fresh black mussels

In a large braising pan, add the olive oil, onion, celery and carrot (soffritto), garlic, hot pepper flakes and optional porcini mushrooms (reserve the water). Over medium heat, cook until the vegetables are soft. If the soffritto threatens to scorch, add a bit of water to the pan.

...continued on page 70

Add octopus pieces to the pan along with the herbs and the kale leaves. Stir and season with salt and pepper as you go. Deglaze the mixture with the wine. Let the alcohol cook off for a couple of minutes, then add the tomatoes, the seafood stock/clam juice, and 2 cups reserved porcini soaking water (add regular water if you didn't soak mushrooms). Reduce heat to low and let cook, covered, about 20 to 25 minutes. (See chef's note.)

When the stew is nearly done, uncover the pan, add the mussels and simmer until they've all opened, 6-8 minutes. (If a mussel doesn't open, do not eat it.)

Serve immediately, accompanied by toasted Tuscan or country-style bread if you like.

CHEF'S NOTE: Talk with your fishmonger about how long to cook the octopus, because the kind you use may change the ideal cooking time. In any case, cook just until tender, testing with a paring knife at the central area of the octopus (the base of the head, where the beak is).

PAPPA AL POMODORO

(TOMATO AND BREAD SOUP)

YIELDS about 8 portions

The idea of pappa al pomodoro is to mix many kinds of tomato products in order to layer tomato flavors. Tomato paste does not taste like fresh tomatoes, which do not taste like canned tomatoes. You can use only canned tomatoes here and the soup will still be good, but try this—the concept of layering flavors is something we do a lot.

A word of caution: Never fill a pot more than halfway with hot oil, and be careful not to put too much bread in the pot, or the oil may overflow. If you don't want to fry, the bread can be toasted in the oven instead.

Canola oil for deep frying

12 cups (1 pound) stale bread, roughly cut into 1-to-2-inch cubes

4 tablespoons extra-virgin olive oil

4 cups (1 pound) onions, sliced

2 sprigs fresh basil

2 sprigs fresh sage

1 3/4 cups (1 pound) canned crushed tomatoes

2 1/2 cups (1 pound) fresh tomatoes, diced

2 tablespoons tomato paste

Salt and pepper

Line a tray with paper towels. Heat a few inches of oil in a large pot to about 325 to 350°F and fry the bread cubes in batches until golden brown. Set aside on the paper-lined tray.

In a large stock pot, add a few tablespoons of olive oil and sweat the onions, without browning, over medium-low heat until soft. Add the fresh herbs to the pot. Then add the canned tomatoes, fresh tomatoes and tomato paste, bring to a simmer and let cook for 10 minutes. Add the bread cubes and let simmer for 5 more minutes. Taste and adjust the seasoning with salt and pepper.

Pappa al pomodoro (like ribollita) is typically better eaten the next day. Reheat to lukewarm and serve topped with fresh olive oil and some grated pecorino or Parmigiano cheese. (Don't tell the Tuscans, they would never forgive you for putting cheese on top of this very traditional soup!)

INSALATA RUSSA

(RUSSIAN SALAD)

YIELDS about 8 one-cup portions

Insalata Russa is often found on cold buffets at parties in Italy. At Papavero it's a handy item to serve on our seafood platter or as one of our "cicchetti" (small bites) during happy hour. For home cooks, it's an easy make-ahead dish for a picnic, and it's great on toast.

The shrimp in this photo are roughly twice the size (U31/35) than the rock shrimp called for, so use whatever you have and chop them if necessary. Rock shrimp are sweeter and more tender. If you're making this for a family and not a party, cut the recipe in half.

3 cups (about 1 pound) red potatoes, diced

4 cups (about 20 ounces) rock shrimp

3 cups spring peas (from frozen; optional)

3 cups mayonnaise or aioli (page 97)

1/2 teaspoon mustard

1/2 teaspoon Worcestershire sauce

1/2 cup (about 2 ounces) scallions, chopped

1 small clove (1/2 teaspoon) garlic, minced

Zest of 1 lime

A few celery leaves, chopped

A pinch of hot pepper flakes

Fine sea salt, to taste

Bring a pot of generously salted water to a boil. Add the potatoes and cook for about 7 minutes. When the potatoes are nearly tender, add the shrimp and continue to cook for 3 to 5 minutes. If using peas, add for the last few minutes of cooking as well. Drain well.

In a large bowl, combine the mayonnaise, mustard, Worcestershire sauce, chopped scallions, garlic, lime zest, celery leaves and hot pepper flakes. Add the shrimp, then fold in the potatoes and peas. Adjust the seasoning with salt if needed. Serve cold.

RAGOUT DI CINGHIALE

(WILD BOAR RAGOUT)

YIELDS about 4 quarts

The recipe is my Uncle Enzo's. He was the hunter of the family. When hunting boar, you never go alone; you need three or four people and multiple dogs. Injured boars can get aggressive, and once caught, they can't be carried alone.

For the restaurant, we get wild boar from Broken Arrow Ranch in Texas, which ships all over the country. This was the only ranch we could find after months of searching that wouldn't send me "fake" boar—pig meat, or boars that were fenced in and fed. What the animal eats makes a big difference in the flavor. There's nothing like boar, but marry pork and beef and imagine something gamey, and that's close.

5 pounds of wild boar, cut into 2-to-3-inch cubes

1 1/2 cup (13 ounces) dry red wine

2 cheesecloth bundles of herbs and spices: rosemary, sage and thyme; cloves, peppercorns and juniper berries (about 2 cups for each bundle)

1 cup extra-virgin olive oil

3/4 cup onion, chopped

1/2 cup carrot, chopped

1/2 cup celery, chopped

1 3/4 cups (1 pound) canned crushed tomatoes

Cooked pasta, polenta, or gnocchi, for serving

The first day, combine the wild boar, the wine (enough to cover the meat), the spices and herbs in a non-reactive container. Cover and refrigerate overnight. The next day, remove the wild boar from the soaking liquid, making sure to save the wine. Pat the meat dry. Discard the used spices and herbs.

In a large braising pan on medium-high heat, sear the wild boar pieces in the olive oil, working in batches so as not to overcrowd the pan. When the boar is browned on all sides, remove it to a plate. Add the soffritto (onion, carrot and celery) to the pan and cook until soft, approximately 3 to 4 minutes, not allowing it to brown. Adding a little water and salt to the pan helps at this stage, as it helps to extract water from the soffritto and prevents it from burning.

Return the boar to the pan, add the reserved wine and cook, giving the alcohol a couple of minutes to evaporate. Add the crushed tomatoes to the pan as well as the fresh bundles of herbs and spices. Season with salt and pepper.

Cover the pan, turn the burner down to low, and let cook for about 3 1/2 hours. Check the pan every hour, as the braised boar might need extra water to prevent it from drying out. When it's done, the boar will be fork-tender (not necessarily shreddable).

Serve the boar with its sauce on your favorite pasta, polenta or gnocchi.

Photo credit: Mike DeVries, Cap Times

Photo credit: Bill Lubing

THE FARMERS' MARKET

MADISON, WISCONSIN

Growing up in San Pietro, the Tuesday morning market was an institution. Stall owners would tour the region with their products, stopping on a designated day of the week in a different town. Each outdoor market was an explosion of smells and colors.

Imagine wood counters set with cases of perfectly arranged vegetables and fruits next to a butcher truck with neatly cut rabbits and chickens. There was a fish guy with local freshwater fish, and saltwater catch from the nearby eastern coast. My mother's favorite was braised tripe and fritto misto from the "fry guy," who also sold doughnuts and bomboloni (**page 55**).

My father grew up in a relatively poor farming family from Puglia in southern Italy, and he knew vegetables pretty well. He had his favorite ones, too: broccoli rabe, fennel bulbs, tomatoes and different kinds of lettuce. (Just don't try to feed him eggplants. Those he despised.)

My dad often reminded me of how, growing up, they ate meat at home only on holidays. He recalled the excitement of being able to eat fish—typically mussels, sardines or anchovies, the cheaper options—on Fridays or Saturdays. What constituted his daily diet during the summer harvesting season? Tomato-rubbed bread and olive oil for breakfast, lunch and dinner. It's not a bad meal, unless that's what you get three times a day!

My father hated to see people being wasteful with food. This stuck with me as I started my career as a professional cook, and it informed the way we use vegetables at Papavero, from leaf to root.

Sometimes, when I go to the farmers' market here in Madison, I have flashes of going to the market in San Pietro in Casale. Some things are very similar, and some things are very different. It's easy to think, "Oh—I was eating this when I was a child," or, "There are eggplants now, so let's make eggplant Parmigiana." Or I see nice tomatoes, so we make a tomato tarragon soup.

I have always loved the Madison farmers' market, but my relationship to the vendors changed in April 2004. I had returned to Madison after two years in Italy, and we now had a 15-month-old child. I knew it would be tough to find a job in a kitchen with an infant at home, so I prepared for the possibility of spending the next 10 to 12 months as a stay-at-home dad.

That's when I met Kay and Paul Jensen from JenEhr Family Farm, a constant presence at the downtown farmer's market on summer Saturdays. We chatted about vegetables, and it turned out that they were looking to hire a chef who could come and cook for their employees during the harvest season—and they didn't mind me bringing along my kid.

I started going to the farm two days a week, cooking from a "mystery box" of ever-changing vegetables, including some odd ones (kohlrabi still looks alien to me to this day). I was used to being surrounded by vegetables. Now I had the privilege of cooking with the very freshest ones.

The menu at Papavero began as the sum of my childhood meals, cooking with my family, as well as my professional influences. I drew from my years cooking in Madison, time in Italy working in restaurants, and one intensive year of studying food and ingredients for my master's degree in Siena—what I think of as the "theory" part.

These were all little pieces of a puzzle, assembled in preparation to one day open my own business. I had experience as a chef and a sous chef. I overlapped childhood experience with professional experience and the master's experience. And by 2006, I was ready to open something.

This section includes dishes that have brought people back to Papavero for years. We have the budino **(page 86)**, or butterscotch pudding, from pastry chef Susan Cesnik. The eggplant caponata **(page 79)** was inspired by Alessandro Monachello, an opening Papavero cook who stayed with the restaurant for well over a decade. The carrot ginger soup **(page 85)** is a recipe I got from chef Jeff Orr, an owner of Cocoliquot and a mentor to me. (Papavero and Cocoliquot shared kitchen space when Papavero opened.)

Sometimes at Papavero I micromanage things, in terms of recipes and cooking times. I can be a little overbearing on the cooks because I want the dishes to taste a certain way, or to have a specific texture. I tell my cooks that the same recipe in each person's hands will come out a little differently. That's one reason they must constantly taste what they're making, checking for enough salt, enough acid, to see if it's cooked through, or if it's too watery or too thick. Tasting and smelling is the most important, in a restaurant and at home.

In Madison, I have found that people validate what we make, especially when they've traveled to or lived in Italy. They understand we do these recipes a certain way—there is a reason for it. And while some of these are restaurant recipes, for the most part, they come from home cooks in Italy. Remember that Italian food is rustic by nature. I hope you enjoy these recipes!

CAPONATA DI MELANZANE

(ALESSANDRO'S EGGPLANT CAPONATA)

YIELDS about 2 quarts

Alessandro Monachello was one of three cooks who helped open Papavero and worked at the restaurant for almost 15 years. He's Sicilian-born and from Palermo, the same hometown as my grandfather on my mother's side. This dish, which frequently shows up on our "verdure" vegetable plate and is wonderful with fish, is a compromise between Alessandro's caponata and the way my grandma used to make it.

My grandma was taught by her sisters-in-law, who were very willing to teach her what my grandfather loved to eat. Alessandro wouldn't put tomato paste in this, but he would use a little cocoa powder to finish, to add a touch of bitterness. That was his secret ingredient.

Canola oil, for frying

1 globe eggplant, about 1 pound, cut into 3-inch cubes

2 1/2 tablespoons extra-virgin olive oil

1/2 medium onion, diced

3 tablespoons capers, drained

1/4 cup diced celery, blanched

3/4 cup (3.5 ounces) good quality olives, pitted and drained

1 tablespoon tomato paste

1/4 cup (2 ounces) apple cider vinegar

1/4 cup (3 ounces) honey

Salt, to taste

Line a tray with paper towels. Heat a few inches of oil to 325 to 350°F in a large pot. Working in batches, fry the eggplant cubes until golden brown. Set on the paper towels and pat dry. Season with salt.

In a medium-sized pan with raised edges set over medium heat, add olive oil, onions, capers and celery. Add a bit of water to the pan if necessary to prevent browning. Once the onion is soft, add the olives, tomato paste, vinegar and honey to the pan. Bring to a simmer, then add the fried eggplants to the pan. Stir well and serve.

Caponata is usually served cold in the summer in Sicily. (It's not served piping hot in the other seasons, either.) Serve with crostini, with fish or as an appetizer on its own.

CHEF'S NOTE: Buy olives already pitted or, for a shortcut, smash them with the bottom of a glass measuring cup or bowl, remove the pits and chop up the rest.

CARBONARA DI PESCE

(SMOKED SEAFOOD PASTA)

YIELDS 3 generous portions

Legend has it that carbonara was named for men who would work in the mines ("carbonaria" are coal miners). It was convenient for them to bring smoked pork and a couple eggs from home, and just make some pasta over a camp stove for their lunch.

At Papavero, we developed this variation for diners who don't want to eat meat. We were already making cured fish, and sometimes we would smoke it to make it last longer. We started swapping fish for the usual guanciale. It's as good as carbonara but without the meat.

8 ounces fresh tagliolini, or your favorite egg pasta

A glug of olive oil

1 small clove (1/2 teaspoon) minced garlic

Freshly ground black pepper

3/4 cup (4 ounces) smoked salmon (or haddock or trout), roughly chopped

5 egg yolks

1 1/2 tablespoons Parmigiano-Reggiano cheese, grated

In a large pot of boiling salted water, cook the pasta according to directions (3 minutes for tagliolini). Reserve some water when you drain it.

In a sauté pan, sweat the garlic in the olive oil along with the black pepper. Add the smoked fish to the pan just to warm up. Next, add the cooked pasta to the pan. Off the stove, add the egg yolks and stir well to combine (be aware that mixing too long can make the egg curdle). Add reserved pasta water if necessary for a rich, silky texture. The pasta should look wet and unctuous, and the eggs should not be scrambled.

Serve immediately, topped with Parmigiano cheese.

CHEF'S NOTE: If you smoke your own fish, a filet is best, and there may be pin bones to remove.

PANINO PAZZO

(CRAZY SANDWICH)

YIELDS 1 sandwich

The name panino pazzo, "crazy sandwich," comes from a pizza place in my hometown. They used to make a sandwich with pizza crust, like a hollow calzone. They'd slice it in half and add a pile of ingredients. There would always be tuna, prosciutto and artichokes, and usually mayonnaise, tomato and lettuce.

The idea is to put many different ingredients you wouldn't think of together in the same sandwich. And it works!

1 ciabatta roll, or another crusty country-style roll, sliced in half lengthwise

2 tablespoons homemade aioli (page 97), **or store-bought mayo**

A few leaves of arugula

4 tablespoons (1.25 ounces) good-quality canned tuna

3 small marinated artichokes, halved

4 thin slices of Italian prosciutto

1 soft-boiled egg (see note), **peeled and halved**

1 slice ripe tomato

Spread the bottom part of the roll with the aioli, then pile up the other ingredients starting with the lettuce, tuna, and artichokes first. Top with the other half of the roll and serve.

CHEF'S NOTE: To soft boil an egg, cook for 6 1/2 minutes in salted boiling water. Drop in cool water to stop cooking, let cool slightly and peel.

PANINO AL PETTO

(BRISKET SANDWICH)

YIELDS 2 sandwiches

This sandwich came about at Papavero because we were already making smoked meats and bacon, and we started applying the same process to brisket. I don't love when a brisket is cooked all the way for hours and hours. Instead we cure it overnight in salt and herbs, then roast it (275°F) until tender and then smoke it.

We were using this brisket on our salumi plate, and I thought, why don't we put it on a sandwich? We sometimes add arugula to this sandwich, and we've been known to put sambal oelek (chili-garlic sauce) on it as well. The onions are saucy enough that it doesn't need more condiments.

1 tablespoon olive oil

1/2 cup red onions, sliced

1 tablespoon apple cider vinegar

Salt, to taste

4 slices of crusty country-style bread

6 slices provolone cheese

1/2 cup pickled goat horn peppers, drained (see note)

10 thin slices of smoked beef brisket

In a frying pan, add the olive oil and set over medium heat. Sauté the onion until soft and translucent, about 10 to 12 minutes. Deglaze the pan with a splash of vinegar. Season the onions with salt and set aside.

Toast the bread slices. Lay the provolone slices on top of two of the warm bread slices, spread the onions evenly over the top, adding the goat horn peppers and brisket slices. Top with the two remaining bread slices. Serve right away.

CHEF'S NOTE: Goat horn peppers are Hungarian, like cayenne peppers but less spicy. They're available to purchase online (mild and spicy) but if you want to pickle peppers on your own, try Carmens. Madison farms are also now growing Jimmy Nardellos, a frying Italian pepper.

ZUPPA DI CAROTE E ZENZERO

(CARROT GINGER SOUP)

YIELDS roughly 8 cups

The years I spent in Madison before opening Papavero were formative because of the chefs I worked with, several of whom became mentors. This recipe comes from Chef Jeff Orr, to whom I'm in debt for the many culinary lessons and recipes he taught me.

This colorful, bright, gingery soup works great in the summer when you have carrots and fresh ginger from the farmers' market, but it's warm and well-suited to winter too.

2 sticks (8 ounces) unsalted butter

1 medium-sized onion, roughly chopped

1/2 teaspoon ground ginger

Kosher salt

4 large carrots (about 1 1/2 pounds), peeled, sliced 1/2 inch thick

4 cups water

1 cup of heavy cream

One 2-inch piece of fresh ginger, peeled and roughly chopped

A splash of apple cider vinegar

Olive oil, fresh chives or croutons, for garnish (optional)

In a large soup pot, melt the butter, then add the onions, dried ginger and a pinch of salt. Cook on medium heat until the onion softens, about 6 minutes. Add the carrots and a pinch of salt and stir.

Add 4 cups of water, to cover. Bring to a simmer and let cook until all the vegetables are soft, about 20 minutes. Add the cream to the pot and bring back to a simmer.

Take the pot off the heat. Add the fresh ginger and blend using an immersion blender, or carefully blend in a blender (drape a towel over the top for protection). The texture should be velvety.

Season the soup with salt and a splash of vinegar, taste to adjust seasoning. Serve warm, garnished with a drizzle of extra-virgin olive oil, minced fresh chives or even some fried bread croutons.

CHEF'S NOTE: For a blended soup, the size of what you cut up at the beginning matters less.

BUDINO DI CARAMELLO

(BUTTERSCOTCH PUDDING)

YIELDS 8 3-ounce portions

Papavero pastry chef Susan Cesnik first spotted this sweet, salty, rich pudding in The New York Times in a 2007 story about Nancy Silverton's Pizzeria Mozza. She adapted Dahlia Narvaez's recipe by adding an extra egg yolk and a vanilla bean to make it richer and more aromatic.

For the best results, have your ingredients measured in advance. Start with the egg mixture, which helps the consistency. This is an excellent dessert to make ahead for a dinner party, as it needs time to set and a small amount goes a long way.

1 whole egg

4 egg yolks

5 tablespoons (40 grams) cornstarch

1 cup plus 2 tablespoons (248 grams) brown sugar

1 1/2 teaspoons kosher salt

1/2 cup water

1/2 vanilla bean, scraped, pod and seeds reserved

3 cups (715 grams) heavy cream

1 1/2 cups (366 grams) whole milk

5 tablespoons (70 grams) unsalted butter, cut into small pieces

1 1/2 tablespoons (21 grams) dark rum, such as Gosling's Black Seal

Dollop of whipped cream and cocoa powder, for serving (optional)

In a large bowl, whisk together the egg, egg yolks and cornstarch until there are no lumps. (Use a whisk attachment on a mixer here if you like.) Set these aside.

In a saucepan, whisk the sugar, salt and water over medium-high heat. Bring this to a simmer and let cook for 5 to 6 minutes. This is your caramel. Add the vanilla bean seeds, pod and cream, then add the milk. Bring back to a simmer, then remove from the heat.

Stabilize the bowl with the egg mixture in it, and ladle about one third of the dairy mixture in, whisking constantly. Once this is well incorporated, add the rest of the dairy mixture, continuing to whisk as you go. You're looking for a light caramel color and a puddinglike consistency. If it's not thick enough, return it to the saucepan and continue to cook over medium heat until it thickens, for just a few minutes.

Remove the saucepan from heat and add the butter and the rum, whisking to combine. Strain through a chinois or fine mesh strainer. Chill until set (at least three hours). Serve with a dollop of whipped cream and sprinkle of cocoa powder.

BUDINO DI CIOCCOLATO

(CHOCOLATE BREAD PUDDING)

YIELDS about 10 portions

We typically make panettone bread pudding at Christmas, but Susan Cesnik decided she wanted to put chocolate bread pudding on the menu about 10 years ago. It's good for guests, because you can make it ahead, slice it and reheat it before serving.

For the best results, make sure the brioche cubes and custard are warm when you combine them, so the bread absorbs the custard better.

1 loaf brioche or 6 buns, cut into cubes

2 1/4 cup heavy cream

1/2 cup milk

1/2 teaspoon vanilla extract

2 pinches of fine sea salt

1 whole egg plus 6 egg yolks

6 tablespoons granulated white sugar

1 1/2 cups (7 ounces) bittersweet chocolate, melted in double boiler/ water bath (see note)

Caramel sauce, raspberry sauce, toasted nuts and/or whipped cream, for garnish

CHEF'S NOTE: Papavero uses 72% dark chocolate, but 60% is delicious as well. Add about 1/2 cup of toasted slivered almonds for a textural contrast.

Preheat your oven to 350°F. Place the bread cubes on a sheet pan and bake for 10 to 15 minutes until lightly toasted. Line a loaf pan with parchment paper.

In a saucepan, heat the cream, milk, vanilla and salt until it comes to a simmer. Meanwhile, put the whole egg, egg yolks and sugar into the bowl of a stand mixer fitted with a whisk attachment. Whisk for a few minutes. Slowly add the scalded dairy. Add the melted chocolate and mix to combine. Set aside.

In a larger bowl, combine the toasted brioche with the chocolate-egg-dairy mixture. Let rest for 4 to 5 minutes. Pour the mixture into your loaf pan, and bake for 25 to 30 minutes, or until set and the pudding starts to pull away from the edges.

Serve the bread pudding warm right out of the oven or chill, cut into slices and reheat to serve. Caramel sauce, raspberry sauce, toasted pecans and/or whipped cream make a nice garnish.

CROSTATA DI PINOLI

(PINE NUT AND HONEY TART)

YIELDS 12 portions

This elegant dessert, a staple at Papavero for at least 10 years, reminds pastry chef Susan Cesnik of honey on toast when she was a kid. It's similar in style to the budino—salty, sweet and buttery—with a lightly crispy crust. Cesnik has made this with chopped pecans in place of pine nuts, and recommends a local honey, like Gentle Breeze.

Use of a scale will make this recipe faster and easier. Depending on the size of your tart pan, you still may have some custard left over. In that case, put it in greased ramekins, top with more pine nuts and bake gently until it's set. It's at its best paired with toasted nuts.

FOR THE DOUGH:

1 2/3 cup (200 grams) all-purpose flour

Pinch of salt

7 tablespoons (100 grams) unsalted butter, cold

2 tablespoons (30 grams) very cold water

1 egg

FOR THE FILLING:

1/2 cup plus 1 1/2 teaspoons (179 grams) honey

1/3 cup plus 1 scant tablespoon (80 grams) sugar

3/4 teaspoon kosher salt

12 tablespoons plus 2 teaspoons (182 grams) unsalted butter

6 tablespoons plus 1 generous tablespoon (95 grams) cream

1 egg

1 1/2 cups (203 grams) pine nuts

Line the bottom of an 11-inch tart pan with parchment paper and spray with nonstick baking spray. Preheat the oven to 350°F.

To make the dough, put the flour and a pinch of salt into a food processor. Cut the butter into chunks and add to the processor. Pulse until it becomes crumbly, like little peas. Add the cold water and the egg and pulse until the dough just starts to pull away from the sides of the bowl. It can be shaggy (lumpy but well-mixed).

Turn out the dough onto a floured surface and work it gently into a ball. Roll it out with a rolling pin until it's an inch or so larger in diameter than your tart pan. Wrap the end of the dough around your rolling pin and lift it into the pan. Fit the dough to the pan fill with pie weights or dried beans and bake for 20 minutes. Remove the beans or weights and return to the oven for 12 to 15 minutes, until golden brown.

Meanwhile, in a saucepan, stir together the honey, sugar, salt and butter over medium heat. Whisk to combine and cook for about 5 minutes until the butter is melted and the sauce is smooth. Remove from heat and let cool for 20 minutes. Add the cream and egg and stir well.

Pour the filling inside the pre-baked tart shell. Top with the pine nuts, spreading them well around. Bake for about 20 minutes or until set. Allow to cool for 2 to 3 hours. You can remove the outer ring after the first hour. Store in the refrigerator. Serve the tart with fresh whipped cream or ice cream on top.

SOUR CREAM ICE CREAM

YIELDS 5 cups

This ice cream was another find by pastry chef Susan Cesnik. It's probably the fastest ice cream ever, because you don't have to make a custard in a bain-marie (water bath), you just mix the ingredients and churn them in an ice cream maker.

While it's one of the fastest ice creams, it's also one of the most delicious. We serve this often with cakes or tarts. It's delicious with a warm brown sugar cinnamon cake (a plum kuchen) with fruit folded into it.

2 cups (1 pound) sour cream

1 cup heavy cream

1/2 cup milk

10 tablespoons white granulated sugar

2 teaspoons lemon juice

1/2 teaspoon vanilla extract

Mix all ingredients with a blender. Churn in an ice cream maker, chill and serve.

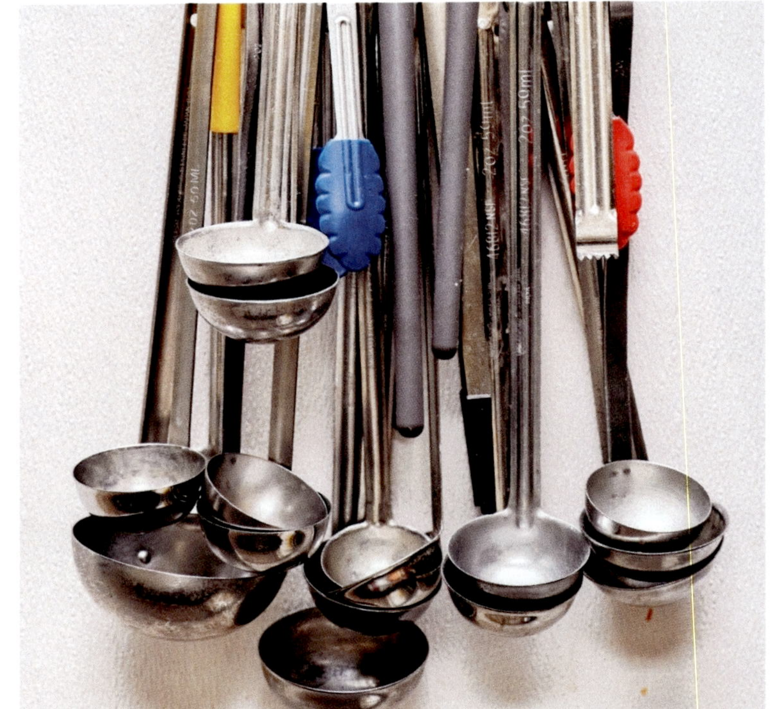

chestnut 8/31
8/31
beets 9/3
chestnut 8/31
broccolini 8/31
sm. beets 9/3
Mush Stew
Pesto 9/1
mushroom stew
pesto

LA DISPENSA

THE PANTRY

These quick little recipes for snacks, dips, vinaigrettes and sauces are often served on the side, or as an accompaniment to other things at Papavero. The tomato sauce and aioli are both base recipes—add to them as you like.

SALSA DI POMODORO

(TOMATO-BASIL SAUCE)

YIELDS approximately 3 cups

This versatile tomato basil sauce finishes many of our main dishes at Papavero—nduja with tagliatelle, eggplant Parmigiana or panzerotti (savory turnovers). It can also be used on its own for a last-minute plate of pasta.

Here we call for Italian canned San Marzano tomatoes. If you adapt it with fresh tomatoes, be sure to consider the water content of the variety you use. Also account for the fact that your sauce may need to be passed through a tomato ricer to remove skins and seeds.

1 28-ounce can whole San Marzano tomatoes

A generous drizzle of olive oil

1/3 teaspoon chopped garlic

1 sprig of fresh basil

Salt

Blitz the tomatoes in a blender until fairly smooth. In a medium-sized soup pot over medium heat, add the oil and sauté the garlic and basil, taking care not to let the garlic brown. Add the tomatoes and the salt. Cook for 20 to 25 minutes. Chill. Will keep in the fridge for 3 to 5 days.

SALSA ROMESCO

(ROMESCO SAUCE)

YIELDS 2 cups

Romesco comes from Catalonia, or the eastern part of Spain. We have sauces that are similar in Italy, that are sweet bell pepper-based. We started using it for the versatility, because it's not too vinegary or salty.

Serve romesco sauce with fish, boiled or grilled meat, bruschetta, even fried eggs. It's good on grilled vegetables too.

3 tablespoons (about 0.75 ounces) plain breadcrumbs

1/4 cup toasted almonds or hazelnuts

Pinch of salt

1 small clove (1/2 teaspoon) garlic

1/4 teaspoon fresh hot chili pepper or sambal oelek

1 tablespoon apple cider vinegar

1 1/2 cups (about 7 to 8 ounces) roasted red bell peppers

2 tablespoons plus 2 teaspoons (1.25 ounces) extra-virgin olive oil

Add the breadcrumbs, nuts, salt and garlic to a food processor and process until smooth. Add the chili pepper, vinegar and peppers to the food processor. Scrape the sides of the bowl to incorporate everything well, and process again until smooth. With the motor running, add the olive oil a bit at a time until well blended. Don't process too long or the sauce will look pink (instead of red). Serve with fish or meat, or on crostini. Keeps for about a week in the fridge.

Photo credit: Shutterstock

SALSA VERDE

(GREEN SAUCE)

YIELDS 2 cups

Salsa verde is one of the most frequently used sauces in Italy, especially in Bologna on bollito misto, the plate served at Christmas with cotechino sausage and capon. It's something I used to eat weekly during the Christmas season.

On the menu at Papavero, we've served this bright-green sauce with everything from beef tongue, pork jowl and seared lamb heart to preserved eggplant and zucchini on our "verdure" (vegetable) plate. We like to serve this with seared beef heart from Cates Family Farm.

If your capers come in a vinegary brine, drain and rinse them. If they come salt-packed, you will need to soak them a couple of times in lots of water. Several herbs work here—try it with mint, basil, dill, tarragon or chervil, or a combination.

2 teaspoons capers

A pinch of hot pepper flakes

2 anchovies in oil, drained

1 small clove (1/2 teaspoon) garlic, roughly chopped

2 tablespoons red wine vinegar

1 1/2 cups (about 3 ounces) packed stemmed Italian parsley, roughly chopped

1/4 cup stale bread, soaked in water 10 to 15 minutes, squeezed out

1/4 cup olive oil

Salt, to taste

In a food processor, combine the capers, hot pepper flakes, anchovies, garlic and vinegar. Purée until fairly smooth. Add the parsley to the food processor along with the bread, and process again. With the motor running, drizzle the olive oil in a steady stream until just combined. Add salt to taste. Adjust the chili and acid to taste. Serve with grilled or poached meats.

AIOLI
(GARLIC MAYONNAISE)

YIELDS about 3 cups

Aioli is made in France, Spain and Italy as well. At the restaurant, we use it on a number of things, including sandwiches, a Russian salad, and on crab slaw for our seafood platter. We make caper aioli to serve with fish. We've added chorizo or tomato—you can go nuts with it.

We never use less than two egg yolks. With those and enough acid, you can make almost a gallon of aioli. Take care not to add the oil too fast or to process too long, as both can make the aioli break (not emulsify). Substitute sunflower or peanut oil if necessary; olive oil can make it taste off or heavy.

2 egg yolks

1 small clove (1/2 teaspoon) garlic, finely minced

2 tablespoons lemon juice

2 tablespoons Champagne vinegar or white wine vinegar

A pinch of fine sea salt

2 cups canola oil

In a food processor, combine egg yolks, minced garlic, lemon juice, vinegar and salt. With the processor on, drizzle the oil in a steady stream. Adjust acidity and salt to taste. The final product should look like a loose mayonnaise. It will keep for about a week.

ACKNOWLEDGMENTS

If this book had even a chance to be written, it is because of many people's hard work and support of Papavero throughout the years. I'm thinking about the many farmers and suppliers that have been part of our journey, our customers, regular and occasional—including all the ones that helped us raise money to keep the business running during the first year of the COVID pandemic. And most importantly all the employees we have had in the past, and the ones we still currently have at the Osteria.

So thank you to the front of the house "backbone": Kevin Trottier, Jaime Blair, Jenny Griep, Stephanie Sudduth, Emily Hatas, Sara Joy Marquez and Marilyn Matt. Thank you to restaurant manager Jonathan Rodriguez, and to Lucas Balamuth, Shooty and Stu Stewart. Thank you to the kitchen "wizards": Miguel Ortega, Alessandro Monachello, Matt Pratt, Charley Becker, Matt Schieble, David Rucinski, Ethan Gillespie and Robert Hughes. And last but not least, thank you to our pastry chef Susan Cesnik.

None of these names are in order of importance, and I am sorry if I left someone off. Thank you all!—Francesco Mangano

Thank you first to Francesco for asking me to work on this project and for your patience with my thousand questions. It has been a joy, and I've learned so much in your kitchen. Thank you to Kristin Mitchell for your wonderful work designing this book, and Sunny Frantz for your beautiful photos. It has been a true pleasure.

Big thanks to our home recipe testers! Ashley, Brett, Gwen, Hywania, Kristina (mom), Lauren, Nate, Nicole, Sarah, Susan and Wendy cooked and tasted these recipes, and gave essential feedback. Especially when something didn't work and we needed to make it better, I was, and am, so grateful for you. Thank you!

Thanks to the staff at Papavero, for your patience and generosity. And thank you Patrick, the best indexer and cat wrangler a person could ask for.

—Lindsay Christians

ABOUT THE AUTHORS

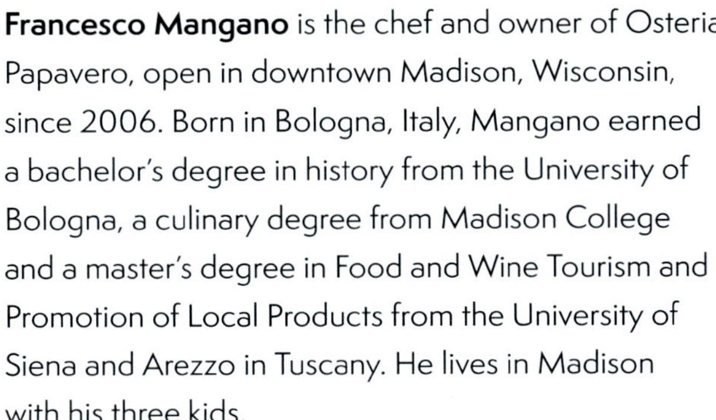

Francesco Mangano is the chef and owner of Osteria Papavero, open in downtown Madison, Wisconsin, since 2006. Born in Bologna, Italy, Mangano earned a bachelor's degree in history from the University of Bologna, a culinary degree from Madison College and a master's degree in Food and Wine Tourism and Promotion of Local Products from the University of Siena and Arezzo in Tuscany. He lives in Madison with his three kids.

Photo credit: Ruthie Hauge

Lindsay Christians is a food editor and arts writer at The Capital Times in Madison, Wisconsin and the author of "Madison Chefs: Stories of Food, Farms and People" from the University of Wisconsin Press (2021). In addition to the Cap Times, her food writing has appeared in Daily Coffee News, Eating Well, Feast & Field, Growler, The Heavy Table and Zagat, among others. lindsaychristians.com

Photo credit: Maureen Janson Heintz

INDEX

Aioli 97

Bechamel sauce 23

Biove Bread 20

Bologna, Italy 10, 12-13, 17, 22-23, 28, 34, 42, 59, 64, 96

Bologna, University of 12

Bolognese Sauce 24

Bomboloni 55

Breads
- Biove Bread 20
- Canederli 50
- Focaccia, Barese-style 18

Bread soup 64

Broken Arrow Ranch 74

Budino di Caramello 86

Budino di Cioccolato 88

Canederli 50

Caponata di Melanzane 79

Carbonara di Pesce 80

Castiglioncello , Italy 10, 17, 59, 68

Cates Family Farm 96

Cesnik, Susan 12, 78, 86, 88, 90, 92

Chocolate roll 40

Cocoliquot 78

Crepes 38

Crespelle 38

Crostata di Pinoli 90

Dessert dishes
- Bomboloni 55
- Budino di Caramello 86
- Budino di Cioccolato 88
- Crostata di Pinoli 90
- Salame di Cioccolato 40
- Sour Cream Ice Cream 92
- Zuppa Inglese 42

Dolomites, Italy 12, 47

Dumplings
- Canederli 50
- Gnocchetti di Patate con Radicchio 34
- Gnocchi di Patate 32
- Gnocco Fritto 22

Eggplant Caponata 79

Eggplant Parmesan 36

Emilia-Romagna, Italy 26, 34

English Trifle 42

Epic Provisions 20

Fennel Gratin 30

Finocchi Gratinati 30

Fish Bresaola 60

Fish, cured 60

Florence, Italy 38, 44, 64

Focaccia, Barese-style 18

Fraboni's 14, 15, 26

Gentle Breeze Honey 90

Glorioso's 14

Goulasch 52

Gnocchetti di Patate con Radicchio 34

Gnocchi di Patate 32

Gnocco Fritto 22

Insalata Rifatta 63

Insalata Russa 72

JenEhr Family Farm 77

Jensen, Kay 77

Jensen, Paul 77

Lasagne alla Bolognese 26

Madison College 12-13

Madison, WI 7, 13, 15, 26, 47-48, 59, 77, 78, 85

Meat dishes
- Goulasch 52
- Insalata Rifatta 63
- Meat Tortelli 28
- Ragout alla Bolognese 24
- Ragout di Cinghiale 74

Meat Tortelli 28

Milwaukee, WI 14

Modena, Italy 14, 34

Monachello, Alessandro 67, 78, 79

Monona, WI 14

Mushroom stew 48

Narvaez, Dahlia 86

Orange Tree Imports 15

Orr, Jeff 78, 85

Palermo, Italy 79

Panino al Petto 83

Panino Pazzo 82

Panzanella 62

Pappa al Pomodoro 71

Parmigiana di Melanzane 36

Pasta Dishes
- Carbonara di Pesce 80
- Lasagne alla Bolognese 26
- Meat Tortelli 28
- Pasta Zucchine e Ricotta 67

Pasticceria Chiari 17
Pisa, Italy 48
Pistoia, Italy 44
Pizzeria Mozza 86
Polenta 57
Potato dumplings 32, 34
Puglia, Italy 18, 77
Ragout alla Bolognese 24
Ragout di Cinghiale 74
Reggio Emilia 14, 34
Ribollita 64
Romesco Sauce 95
Salads
 Insalata Rifatta 63
 Insalata Russa 72
 Panzanella 62
Salame di Cioccolato 40
Salsa di Pomodoro 94
Salsa Romesco 95
Salsa Verde 96
San Pietro, Italy 12, 17, 22, 77
Sauces
 Aioli 97
 Bechamel Sauce 23
 Ragout alla Bolognese 24
 Ragout di Cinghiale 74
 Salsa di Pomodoro 94
 Salsa Romesco 95
 Salsa Verde 96
Seafood dishes
 Carbonara di Pesce 80
 Fish Bresaola 60
 Zimino di Cozze 68
Siena, University of 13
Silverton, Nancy 86
Slow Food 13
Soups/Stews
 Goulasch 52
 Pappa al Pomodoro 71
 Ribollita 64
 Zimino di Cozze 68
 Zuppa di Carote e Zenzero 85
 Zuppa di Funghi 48
Sour Cream Ice Cream 92
Tomato-Basil Sauce 94
Trentino, Italy 32, 47, 52, 57
Tuscany, Italy 10, 44, 48, 62, 64, 68
Tyrol, Italy 47, 52
Vegetable dishes
 Caponata di Melanzane 79
 Finocchi Gratinati 30
 Parmigiana di Melanzane 36
 Pasta Zucchine e Ricotta 67
 Zucchine Ripiene 44
Zimino di Cozze 68
Zucchine e Ricotta Pasta 67
Zucchine Ripiene 44
Zucchini, stuffed 44
Zuppa di Carote e Zenzero 85
Zuppa di Funghi 48
Zuppa Inglese 42

Printed in the United States
by Baker & Taylor Publisher Services